MW00965305

Tales of a Mermaid Gone Over The Deep End

Sue,

Thank you for going Over The Deep End with me! ♡

Teresa Fischtner

Teresa Fischtner

Tales of a Mermaid Gone Over The Deep End
Copyright © 2021 by Teresa Fischtner

All rights reserved. No part of this publication may
be reproduced, distributed, or transmitted in any
form or by any means, including photocopying,
recording, or other electronic or mechanical
methods, without the prior written permission of
the author, except in the case of brief quotations
embodied in critical reviews and certain other
non-commercial uses permitted by copyright law.

Tellwell Talent
www.tellwell.ca

ISBN
978-0-2288-6300-7 (Paperback)
978-0-2288-6301-4 (eBook)

Tales of a Mermaid Gone Over The Deep End

Hello friend, and welcome to my life. If you're reading this book, you might already know me, and if you know me, there is a chance you're in this book. Don't worry; names and nipples have been changed for our protection.

This is a feel-good book of *true* short stories about me, my family, friends, and my aqua fit business, Over The Deep End. We all have stories to share, and the true ones are always the best. My mom was a fabulous storyteller, and I inherited that gene. My dad was the most generous man I know, and yes, I got the jackpot on that one too. I'm sharing some of my most vulnerable moments, some of my greatest moments, and some of my saddest. Tears are tears. Happy or sad—we all feel. In your hands isn't just a book, it's me: the good, the bad, the funny. Hopefully, in one story or another, you find something way better than me—you might find you. We all have a story and a different way to tell it. I hope telling my stories helps you tell some of your own.

Happy Reading!

Table of Contents

To all the Mermaids I've Loved Before...

I dedicate this book to my husband Ron for making me laugh every day (often without him even noticing). Ron has stood cover in front of me for my worst moments, behind me when it was my turn to shine, and right beside me for the last thirty-five years.

My son Ronny and his partner Michelle (hopefully fiancée by the time this book gets printed) for being a quiet, respectful wall of support when I need someone to lean on.

My daughter Malyn for never doubting me or letting me doubt myself. This little lady reminds me every day what girl power feels like, and it feels awesome!

These are the people that gave me all the room I needed to be the best me I can be (and have provided most of the material for this book!). It's easy to love your family, but liking them takes commitment and a strong sense of self. We all work together, live next door to each other, and still sit down together for dinner on Sundays. Our fortune is the sum of all our parts; yes, we look like we're on the Crazy Train, and together we have the strength of a locomotive.

There is one other person that I dedicate this book to, Monica Bos.

When we are young, we are told we can be anyone and do anything we want. As we get older, we stop hearing that; we start to hear "what" we are good at and how to make a career or a life from that. At my last accounting job, I worked with Monica. She retired, and I inherited her position in her family business. When I left that career to pursue aqua fit, I told her my plans for the pool and that I was scared it would be an epic failure. She looked me in the eye, held my hand in hers, and Monica said:

"You are the kind of woman that can do *anything* you want to do."

That's a powerful sentence, but without Monica, it's just words. She honestly believed it, and she made me believe it too.

How lucky was I to have a friend that believed in me wholeheartedly, and how lucky was she to have the courage to say it? Women lifting, inspiring, encouraging, and challenging each other—it has nothing to do with luck; that's woman's liberation. Now that I know I can do anything, I want to be a woman that can tell her friends the same: You can do anything you want.

Please, Please Write a Book!

Let's be honest, we all think we can write a book, right? So, what stops us? Self-doubt? Your friends finding out you're a dumb ass? Our jobs, aka—mortgage? No publisher? Never thought that far? Honestly, me neither. I couldn't get past my friends finding out I'm a dumb ass.

What every writer needs is a captive audience. No better way to capture an audience than to shut down the economy, the entertainment industry, close the gyms, pools, theatres, concerts—hell, let's go all the way—no shopping! Enter stage left: COVID-19. First of all, if you lost someone to this virus, I'm sorry. I really am. A global pandemic is not something to be made light of, and I'm not doing that. I'm the eternal optimist. COVID-19 was terrible, and it taught all of us things about ourselves we needed to learn.

I was running my aqua fit business, Over the Deep End, when the pandemic hit and I was closed. We have a little community of aqua fitters that were thrown out of the pool and we had to learn to swim on land. I started a little blog called Daily Love; I sent it to my customers, and posted it to my Facebook page. It started as a short-term fix to keep my ladies moving (motion is the lotion), but this freaking virus lasted long and came back for more than one repeat performance. My blog became my diary, my diary became my purpose, and my purpose was making people smile without trying to sell anything and no bullshit!

So great was my blog, that everyone was *begging* me to write a book. OK, so to keep it bullshit-free, only four people asked me to write a book, and only three of those four said they would buy it. With my ego hungry and my audience captive, my book was started.

This isn't a self-help or self-discovery book; these are just stories, true and told by me with a pinch of humour, a handful of humble, and a dash of fear. Keep a glass of water (wine) and some Pepto Bismal (Kleenex) nearby; you might need it. If I wrote this book the way I intended, it should feel like a hug. The pandemic kept us apart and made us want to get closer than we've ever been. Open your mind and embrace mine, and let's reconnect one page at a time.

How to Read this Book

I've read a lot of books, and I hate it when I open a book, and they start with a chapter called How To Read This Book. Does the author think I'm a complete idiot? Why would I buy a book if I didn't know how to read the damn thing? Seriously, who needs to be told *how* to read a book? Sadly, my friend, you do. Not because you don't know how to read a book, but because I don't know how to write one. Let me explain, and I'll keep it simple in case there are, in fact, any actual "idiots" that bought this book.

The stories in this book span my fifty-plus years. Some of those years and characters didn't make the book. Think of the Toronto Maple Leafs; no one needs to re-live their last fifty years. All you need is the highlights reel. Now, in the case of the Leafs, that would make a *very* short high lights reel. Luckily my team has more talent and a lot more wins. Neither of us is likely to ever win the Cup, and yet every day, we face off with anyone willing to play with us.

I've written about blocks of my life, and to piece them all together, I've included a few "Life Bridges." These life bridges are for you to have some sense of chronological order to my ramblings. So that's how you read this book, enjoy it story by story and cross the bridges when you come to them.

To start you on the right path, here is your first bridge to cross; it will take you from the early '70s right into the start of the twenty-first century.

You are going to quickly learn about me growing up and some of my firsts. In just a few short chapters, you will meet my parents, walk awkwardly with me through adolescence all the way down the aisle to matrimony and right into the joys of raising children and the gut-retching pain of grief. Buckle up; it's a rough and windy road on this first leg of the trip.

My Best Friend is a Bitch

I know what you're thinking: *What kind of person would call her best friend a bitch, and make it the title of a chapter in her book?* Seriously though, more often than not, when my friend's name is mentioned, it's followed by "is a bitch." Let me explain.

I was born the youngest of five kids. I have three sisters and one brother. My parents were Dutch immigrants who worked hard building up their farm and raising their family in rural Ontario. I had a good family, good friends, and a good education. I was one of the lucky ones, or was I? Of course I was. Wasn't I?

When I had a scratch ticket as a teenager, I honestly believed that if I scratched it in a certain order and really concentrated on winning, then I would have a winning ticket. If I won anything, it meant I was doing it right. If I lost, it meant I did it wrong. There was no such thing as a losing ticket, only a loser scratching a ticket. Oh, the pressure I was living under to think my thoughts and my efforts controlled everything that happened; it was a lot.

I could always attribute bad things happening to me as being "my fault," while good things happened out of luck. As I got older and more comfortable in my own skin, I realized not everything was a natural consequence of what I did or what I thought. There was something else at play in my life, and I was equally relieved by it as I was scared of it. I didn't have to right all the wrongs in life; sometimes, they would right themselves. I didn't need to judge other people, and in turn, I didn't feel judged myself. I finally found a belief system that I could believe in; her name is Karma.

I believe Karma is everywhere. She is rewarding good deeds and challenging the wrong. Karma is the belief that good things happen to good people and bad things happen to bad people. My Karma is a little different, and sometimes bad things happen to good people. Sometimes it's hard to know the difference; some of the most challenging times in my life I can look back on now with awe. I can see how getting through pain has made me more empathetic, being broke has made me generous, and being sick has made me health conscious. As for bad things happening to bad people, I don't believe there are bad people. We are all born with the same abilities to love, be kind, forgive, and nurture. Every day we choose to use those gifts that we were born with or not. Don't get me wrong; my rose-coloured glasses haven't blinded me. No one can get through life being a prick without getting pricked. But in general, people are good and what comes around goes around, and that's really good.

Karma is my best friend, and yes, she can be a bitch. She is my ride or die, and she always steers me in the right direction. In reading this book, you might mistakenly think

Karma has been really good to me to have all these great people and opportunities in my life. I'm not pretending my life is all rainbows and lollipops; that's what Facebook is for! My life isn't perfect, but I'm writing this book to make you smile and maybe even laugh out loud. As for the bad stuff that is part of my life? I'm taking a lesson from my dog Wally, just kick some dirt over that shit and carry on.

Home is Where the Heart is...

I have to start with my parents' love story. My dad's family of ten immigrated to Canada. He was the oldest and came here on his own to scout out a homestead (I know it sounds corny, but no shit, that's what he did). When his family was here and settled, he went back to Holland to find a wife. Back then, Canada did not have an ample supply of Dutch women. Luckily the early immigrants reproduced like rabbits, and now we have *plenty*.

He met my mom, and they fell in love. It was a bonus that she had a sister for one of Dad's cousins, and he had a sister for one of Mom's cousins (again, no shit, true story; big families were the first version of Tinder). My mom's family was all in Holland, and she would be leaving everyone behind. My grandfather gave them his blessing and some very important advice for my dad. He told him that my mom would be homesick and that under *no* circumstances can she come back to Holland in the first six months. No matter how much she wanted to, she couldn't come home, and if they could make it through that, they would be fine.

My mom cried every day for six months. Her homesickness made her feel colder than our frigid Canadian winters, and it made her stronger than any woman I've met. She wanted to go home more than anything she'd ever wanted in her life. When the time and finances allowed them to go back to Holland for a visit, they were both afraid leaving would be hard again. After weeks with her family, it was time to go home, and my mom wanted to go home—she had made her peace with a new country, new language, and new family, all made possible with new love. Her home was in Canada.

One of my favourite childhood memories of my mom is of every Saturday night when she would sit at the kitchen table with rollers in her hair, re-read her letters from her sisters, and write her own letters back to them. She would translate for us summaries of what was in the letters. They made the ordinary sound exciting, and all the sisters had a funny bone that made those letters worth gold in each other's hands. There are lots of love stories about finding a partner, but keeping a family's love together over a lifetime and an ocean apart are few and far between. That's my parents' love story; they never divided their love—they multiplied it. Their love was always just a postage stamp away.

First day of High School

Everyone remembers their first few days of high school, some fondly, others (me) not so much. I was always anxious as a kid. These days, anxiety and panic attacks are common and openly addressed. Back in my day, we didn't talk about how we felt. We just felt it until we blacked out—that was me, the fainter. I was nervous about starting high school. It was big with 2000-plus students, and like every thirteen-year-old girl, I wanted to be accepted (aka, hugely popular!).

The last class of the day for me was gym (ugh). I was never an athletic kid, and by that, I mean I was *really* bad. To make matters worse, the girls' change room was in the basement. It was way too small with low ceilings, and it was crowded. I think everyone has a bit of claustrophobia, and some of us have *a lot*.

First day, last class, hot September day; it was a stressful time in deed. Thank goodness it was an all-girls class, so at least I didn't have any jocks to humiliate myself in front of, and I had two of my best friends with me! We all got dressed and went outside to the track; warm-up was a one-mile run. OMG. By that, I mean, *oh my god, that is bat shit crazy!* I don't run; I don't jog; I walk only when I have to. It was a quarter-mile track, so that meant four times around it for a mile. I was freaking out, but I'm an optimist. Maybe I can run; I had never really tried to run a mile, so, hey, maybe it's not that bad. *Running is bad!* I made it around once and had to drop it to a walk for the second lap. Third round, I made a pathetic attempt at a jog, and by the final round, I was the only one still out on the track. My two best friends came back for me, and each hooked an arm in mine and literally dragged me the last quarter mile. It was clear; I didn't know how to run, but I was awesome at picking friends.

For the rest of that class, all I can remember is trying to recover and how I would convince my parents that a spare this semester would serve us all much better than this shit. The class ended late, and all the girls had to rush to the change room to get changed in time to catch our busses. If you were a farm kid, catching the bus was crucial. Farm parents didn't taxi their kids around; they just didn't, and kids just knew it. There were thirty-plus girls in this tiny change room, all frantically getting changed after completing a near marathon. This was not my happy place, not at all.

I felt dizzy and hot. I thought, *shit, if I faint now, I am going to miss my bus for sure.* Next thing I know, I am half-dressed, propped up against the cement wall with my phys ed teacher (a man no less; exactly what every thirteen-year-old girl needs!) taking my pulse.

Phys ed teacher: Hey wake up; you're fine, it's okay. Does anyone know her name?

I did wake up. I was fine, and yes, I missed my frigging bus.

First Date Fiasco

This is all true (sadly). There was no crossing of oceans or love at first sight, just a comedy of errors. Go get your Kleenex and stretch your abs; some serious belly laughs are coming at you.

Ron, my first husband—he is my only husband, but I like to say "first husband" to keep him on his toes—and I met casually at a party and exchanged phone numbers, actual land line phone numbers (remember those?) He called the next day and asked me on a date for the following weekend, dinner at the Black Angus and drinks at a bar in London. I was all of sixteen years old, but with three older sisters, a fake ID could always be found (stolen). The day before our date, he called and asked if I could drive. You see, he had no car, and, oh ya, his license was under suspension (ya, I know winner-winner chicken dinner; but wait, it gets better). I was a gracious young girl, so of course, I agreed to drive.

I went to pick up my twenty-three-year-old date where he lived with his parents (red flag number two for those of you counting), and he asked me to pull the car around the back and reverse up to the wooden shed at the very back of the property. This is where I drew the line. You see, I'd just got my driver's license, and I wasn't that good at backing up—he would have to back up the car himself! At the shed, he popped the trunk and proceeded to fill the hatch of my four-door Chevette with cases upon cases of empty beer bottles. Once the car was loaded (and smelled like an empty beer bottle), off we went to Brewers Retail. He had bottle money to collect! (ya, I know; red flag number three.) With money in his pocket and gas in my car, we went for dinner. Thankfully his bottle collection covered our dinner check (I avoided appetizers to play it safe). The night was young, and so were we. The Ox Box in London was a hot spot with live entertainment. With fake ID in my wallet, we were good to go.

There was a line up for the bar and a cover charge of ten dollars per person. (You know where this is going, don't you?) Ron had enough for the cover but asked if I could buy the drinks (I know flag number four—don't judge me, I was only sixteen years old!). We got in the bar. It was so crowded and billowing with smoke. (Can you imagine smoking indoors?!) We found a table, and Ron was off to the bar to get us drinks with my twenty bucks. It was so crowded and hot, and I'm a fainter—always have been and probably always will be. I have a long list of places I've fainted: bank, post office, vet, Disney Land, CN tower, you name it. When I feel crowded in, I kiss the carpet. Well, I was very crowded in at the bar, and that floor was gnarly; I was not going down on that—I do have some standards (just not when it comes to dates). I found Ron at the bar. I told him I was going to faint and we needed to leave.

Ron: Just wait a minute, he's bringing me my change.

(Ya, I know—that was *my* change.) I explained that we had to go right *now*, a lifetime of fainting gives you the advantage of knowing how long you have, and I didn't have time to wait for the change. Ron looked for the bartender, and in that instant, I was down. I woke up on the sidewalk outside with a 400-pound bearded bouncer asking how old I was.

We made it back to the car and sat there until I felt well enough to drive again (remember, I'm still on a date with a hobo). We made it back to Strathroy; I dropped him off and went home myself incident-free.

You're probably wondering how we got from there to here, and you romantics are hoping I write about patience, kindness, love, and understanding. (Spoiler alert: that's not it!) My single most favourite thing to do in life is laugh, and yes, he could barely buy me dinner, he didn't own a car or a valid driver's license, but there has rarely been a day in the last thirty-five years that he didn't make me laugh.

My Wedding Dance with Paul Anka

After five years of dating and living in sin, Ron found (drank) the courage to ask my parents for my hand in marriage (and they say chivalry is dead). My parents gave him their blessing, and three days later, on Valentine's Day, he almost proposed.

For Valentine's Day, he gave me a beautiful jewellery box; I thought the box was the gift, and I loved it!

Ron: No, open it.

Inside was another beautiful box—I loved that too!

Ron: No, open it.

There was the ring, sparkling with life. I looked at him, expecting him to ask me something.

Ron: Don't you think it's about time?

It took another six years to get me down the aisle, so apparently, it wasn't "about time" for me.

I didn't want a big wedding, and my dad didn't want a small wedding; that meant no wedding for a long time, eleven years to be exact, but who was counting? I really wanted to elope, and I had Ron convinced it was a good idea, but he insisted that we tell our parents. We agreed that he would tell my parents, and I would tell his parents (I was getting a really sweet deal on this and he was getting screwed, hard). We started with my parents. He practiced what to say, how to lead into it, and how to convince them it was a good idea. He was ready! I called and asked if we could come over on a Friday night (highly unusual for us). We arrived on time (also highly unusual for us), we sat down, and Ron talked about everything under the sun while I sat beside him, not saying a word (highly unusual for me). We left two hours later without a single word of marriage or eloping ever spoken. My parents were completely baffled by our visit, and Ron was exhausted from running circles around the conversation we never had.

There was no way Ron was going to elope without telling my parents, and there was no way he could break it to them. Eventually, my dad realized the only way he was going to walk his last daughter down the aisle was if he agreed to a small wedding. Immediate family only with a couple special aunts and uncles—the date was set. I bought the first wedding dress I tried on, booked the hall, called the priest and asked my mom to make her famous roast beef and Ron's mom to make her mouth-watering schnitzel—we were going to the chapel, my style! All the arrangements were made by September, and we would be married the following March. Sweet and simple, no surprises, exactly the way I liked things. We only forgot to send one invitation, and as luck would have it, it was the one for Karma.

What's the difference between a surprise and a shock? A little pink line on a pregnancy test is the difference. Ron and I were not planning to start a family; hell, it took us eleven years to set a wedding date. We had tons of nieces and nephews; we didn't need any kids of our own. Our siblings were more than happy to lend out theirs, and we were more than happy to take and return them.

How did I get pregnant? Well, this isn't that kind of book. I'm assuming you already know how that happens. Just call me Fertile Myrtle. I was on birth control pills, but I had the flu, and for over a week, I couldn't keep anything down. My doctor explained it could be as simple as throwing up my pills or having been on them too long—they were less effective. Either way, the four pregnancy tests I took were all right. I was definitely pregnant.

We decided to keep the news to ourselves until after the wedding. We both needed time to process this. Honestly, after eleven years together, what were the chances that I would get pregnant three months before our wedding? Karma—that bitch!

We were getting married in a church, so we had to tell our priest; correction, Ron had to tell our priest (I'm fine with little white lies, and I was only a couple of months along, so technically, the lie was still very little). We were expecting fire and brimstone and bible scripture that would put us to shame. Kudos to our priest. He congratulated us and agreed to keep it quiet. He said most couples he counselled didn't stay married as long as we had already been together. He assured us we could handle this. He thanked us for our honesty and gave us a hug. Oh, my sweet Karma.

We wanted to tell everyone in our families at the same time and decided the best time to do that was at the wedding. I arranged it with our DJ the night before our wedding that he would announce that we had some news to share, and we wanted to do it with a song. Ron and I got on the dance floor, and he played Paul Anka's song, "Having My Baby." It was very quiet for the first verse, and by the second chorus, there was cheering and clapping.

Having my baby, what a lovely way of saying how much you love me?

My Dad

My Dad was awesome. He was a farmer, a businessman, an inspiration to many people, and a cracker jack of a prankster.

April fool's day was his calling. One year for April first, he asked my sister Mary to go to the co-op to buy a sky hook for him. There is no such thing as a sky hook, and perhaps the name should have been her first clue, but honestly, who would've thought there is really a tool called bullnose pliers, and there is, so don't judge her. Dad called the co-op and asked them to play along and tell her they sold out, but she could get one at the TSC. Then he called the TSC and asked they do the same thing but send her to the UAP, and then he called the UAP... Each store she went to had a little more fun messing with her. Mary came home after hours of searching for a sky hook, furious that this little town we lived in didn't have a single sky hook in it! Dad laughed all day long.

We lived on a farm, and dad ran a dead stock removal business. Most of you won't know what that is, and there are very few left these days, but they were an important part of the farming industry at one time. Grinsven Stock Removal picked up dead animals from farms for processing. These are animals that died of natural causes, nothing that would ever end up on your plate, but quite likely in your dog or cat's bowl. Farmers would call us when they had dead animals, and the drivers would go from farm to farm, picking up dead cows and pigs and, lucky for me, the occasional horse.

A call came in from a lady that was moving from the country to the city; she had a horse that couldn't come with her and no one to take the horse. Calling my dad to dispose of it was more cost-effective than calling a vet. She asked if there was an extra charge for shooting it and if it could be taken off her property alive and then dealt with elsewhere? Well, of course, that could be arranged, and it just so happened that her call came in a week before my birthday—Karma? (Spoiler alert: Karma has a thing with horses in my family.) I know when you think of little girls that got ponies for their birthdays, it makes you want to gag a little, but trust me, I wasn't that kind of little girl, and this was no pony! The horse was pure black, and I named her Midnight; she was broken but preferred to be ridden bareback. She was very slow unless she got spooked, and then she was very, very fast. She lived in the barn with a couple of hundred beef cows. She was really everyone's horse, but I can always say my dad got me a pony for my birthday when I was a little girl.

My dad was traditional; he was the man of the house, but he was ahead of his time, seeing only strength in women, not weakness. He encouraged my mom to get her driver's licence even though most of her friends hadn't. He celebrated her success by buying her a Chevrolet Vega. In her eyes, that Vega was a Rolls Royce, a pure luxury that showered her with independence. He encouraged all four of his daughters to go to college, start their own business, manage their own finances, and be independent. My brother Murray was his right and sometimes left hand, too; he took over the farm.

Dad was very generous of his time and his resources; it came naturally to him. He was also painfully empathetic. During my first pregnancy, I was having nightmares about giving birth. I didn't want to do it. Don't get me wrong. I wanted that kicking, nauseating bundle of sleepless nights out of me. I just didn't want to give birth to it. I wanted a c-section. I talked to my doctor, who suggested I start hypnosis to calm my fears. My mom was a midwife. She knew I would be fine and kept telling me so.

My Dad wanted me to have whatever I wanted to have (like a pony for my birthday!). He went to my doctor's office, where he was not a patient and did not have an appointment. He wanted to talk to my doctor, and he would sit and wait until he saw him. Sit and wait, he did, for hours, until eventually, my doctor tired of the receptionist asking, "What are we going to do with this guy? He won't leave." Dad wanted to get me a c-section. He asked my doctor to promise me a c-section to put me at ease and bill him directly so as not to abuse OHIP. My doctor tried to explain that vaginal birth was so much better for both mom and babe, but I was both mom and babe in Dad's eyes, and his little girl wanted a c-section. Neither my mom nor dad told me about his visit to my doctor's office. I found out about it at my next check-up. That made for a tearful conversation with my doctor, who was also a father himself and understood that kind of love.

My son, Ronny, was born a few months later and after thirty hours of labour, guess what I got, a cesarean. Never ever wish for a c-section; lesson learned, lady Karma. My mom and dad were the first ones at the hospital. I think my dad would have just as soon swaddled me in a blanket and held me on his chest, but that wasn't going to happen. He was proud of me, and I had the finest example of good parents right there in front of me.

Ten months later, he had a heart attack; his steps to heaven were the first cracks of my heart. There are no words to tell you how much I miss my dad, but there are millions of words to share the memories of my dad, and for that, I'm grateful.

Can We Get Turtles Now?

My mom was the most vibrant, resilient, funny woman I have ever known. She was quick-witted and made everyone laugh. She told the funniest stories and always had a glass-half-full attitude. She was an incredible woman and set the bar high for her five kids to rise up to.

She fought her way through bone cancer as a child, through breast cancer as a young woman, and through thyroid cancer later in life. She was one tough cookie. She was always active; she cut her grass with a push mower for the exercise of it, she babysat her twelve grandchildren and hosted all the family gatherings herself. Yup, she was Super Mom. Then she had a stroke.

Her first stroke was what they call a "warning." It had only slightly affected her leg, and that recovered not long after it happened. It gave us all a scare, but we were sure it was a one-and-done. She was only seventy-two and in great shape. A few weeks later came her second stroke. This one was not as forgiving as the first. It went on like that for a couple of months; every few weeks, she would have another stroke that would affect a different part of her body or her mind. One of her strokes affected her speech, not the drooped mouth you associate with strokes. It was her language. I would walk into her hospital room and have these bizarre conversations.

Me: Hi Mom, how are you today?

Mom: Green Nunavut ice cream door.

In her mind, she answered my question. She smiled back at me to reassure her that I had heard her correctly. She called us by the wrong names, or not even by names. I brought in the scrapbooks I made for her over the years. I would point out her in the pictures, and she took a pen and drew arrows to those pictures and wrote "me."

It was heartbreaking. Every time she had a stroke, it was like a punch in the gut to our family, and then a few days later, she would rally back a bit, and we thought, *OK, she can live with this. We will adapt things for her*, and then another stroke and another punch to the gut. My kids were four and six, a very young age to understand what was going on. Ron's dad had passed away just one month before my mom's first stroke. This was a lot for our young little family to handle. I was spending most of my time at the hospital with my mom, and Ron was still grieving his dad and caring for his mom. The only thing our kids wanted was turtles; yes, two turtles. They had been asking for turtles for months, and we didn't need extra pets to care for while Ron's dad was sick, so I kept putting them off. Then without skipping a beat, my mom was sick, so I kept saying, when Oma gets better, we will get turtles then, I promise!

Oma didn't get better. She continued to have strokes every few weeks over four months. That sounds terrible, and it was, but there were some shining moments. She was in Parkwood for a few weeks and had wonderful care; we had lots of quality visits with her. She even made a run for it once. She managed to slip out of her wing and down the elevator to get out to the garden on her own. There was an incident of chocolate-milk-stealing from another patient. That gave us all a chuckle. She was still Super Mom, but her super powers had changed from witty words to surviving strokes.

In the end, she did come home again and had all her family with her. It was terrible and beautiful, heartbreaking and life-changing.

I called Ron to let him know mom had passed away and asked that he tell the kids on his own. I had done the same for him just a few months earlier when his dad passed. We both knew the speech, and the kids were so young they couldn't grasp what had happened, no matter how they were told. After the funeral and things had settled down, I finally asked Ron how the kids reacted.

Ron: Oh, you know how kids are. They don't understand.

That meant they said something he didn't want to tell me. I pushed, and finally, he shared what happened. He told them Oma went to heaven to be with Grandpa, and there she would be better and happy. He reassured them that everything would be fine and asked if they had any questions.

Ronny: Can we get turtles now?

Malyn: Mom promised turtles when Oma was better, two turtles.

I love resilience. I picked the kids up after school the day Ron told me this, and we went turtle shopping!

Damn turtles. Ugh, first of all, they start very small and very cute. They are fairly easy to care for: a tank, some rocks, a little food, easy stuff. What you don't know is they grow fast, and the bigger they get, the more they poop. I mean, they poop all day, every day—it doesn't stop, and it *stinks*. You have to clean the tank every other day, and if you don't, you will gag every time you go past them.

As the turtles got bigger, the kids lost interest in playing with them. Here I was, stuck with two turtles that did nothing but eat and poop and stink up my family room. Too big to flush down the toilet! Damn turtles.

I had a friend whose son was into all kinds of fish and reptiles. He had the basement of their house full of tanks. I asked if he might like a couple of turtles to add to his collection, tank and all the supplies included, *free*! I was honest about their personal hygiene and toileting issues. She laughed and said, "Yeah, no problem. Bring them over." Bingo! The kids said goodbye to Matts Sundin and Anabella (you can probably guess whose was whose). I brought the smelly beady-eyed creatures to my friends' business; her husband was there and said he knew about the turtles and would bring them home that night.

A year later, I saw my friend again and asked about the turtles. Her husband did bring them home that night as he said he would. He put them in the corner of the garage with the intention of having his son get them later. We all know the road to hell is paved with good intentions. A few weeks later, they noticed a bad smell in their garage. They washed the garbage cans, and the smell got worse. They set mouse traps, and the smell got worse. The smell became unbearable. They emptied out the entire garage, and there sat Matts Sundin and Anabella, still alive and pooping!

I think my mom heard my kids asking if they could get turtles now that Oma was better in heaven. I'm sure she was shaking her head with a smile on her face while I bought the turtles. I'm certain she was laughing wholeheartedly every time I washed their stinking tank. I'm positive she was elbowing my dad, pointing, and belly laughing when they were finally set free in my friends' pond.

Damn turtles!

Barney in Buckhorn

I don't talk a lot about my in-laws without checking over both shoulders and dropping my voice to a whisper, just joking (kind of). This is the story that I like to remember my father-in-law by.

My mother-in-law lived in the former Yugoslavia with her very poor family while it was still a communist country. She fled her country on foot in the dark and ran to neighbouring Austria. She found a job cleaning rooms in a hotel and found other refugees to live with in the basement of that hotel. My father-in-law was a truck driver and delivered fruit to that hotel. They met there while he was delivering fruit. The kids and I laughed until we cried when Josephine (my mother-in-law) told us this story in her still-very-thick accent.

Josephine: I couldn't believe it, I never in my life saw a banana, and he had such big beautiful banana

He won her over with a banana! He romanced her with fresh fruit she never tasted in her own country or even knew existed. They married and immigrated to Canada a year before my parents. Life wasn't always kind to them, but their love raised a family to be proud of.

My father-in-law, George, taught my son Ronny the pride of hockey, and my son taught my father-in-law what total admiration feels like. Grandpa George lived, loved, and cheered the Toronto Maple Leafs and when the game was on, the only thing that could interrupt it was a big purple dinosaur.

We took Ron's parents for a vacation to Buckhorn. Our son Ronny was just over a year old, and I was seven months pregnant with Malyn; good times for sure (not!). We booked a cottage at Beachwood Resort in Northern Ontario (look them up—totally worth it!). We had a small lakeside cottage for the May long weekend.

Humble took a step up in my character to see how much my mother-in-law, Josephine, enjoyed cottage housekeeping and meals at the lodge. She was so proud that her son had taken her on this trip, and everyone at the lodge had to hear about it; it was really sweet.

It was the Stanley Cup playoffs. Your first question is obvious: *Hockey in May? WTF!?* Hockey is for fall and winter, not spring and summer—this was bullshit! I was in Northern Ontario during playoffs with a hockey family. How did a smart, independent woman put herself in such a precarious situation? Hormones, you idiot! I was pregnant a second time and totally messed up.

My little Ronny bear fell asleep every night watching a Barney video snuggled up with his red-and-white stripped baby blanket. It was 7:30 p.m.; bedtime was 8:00. There was only one TV, and the Leafs were playing (and probably losing). Ronny was craving that big purple dinosaur, like any two-year-old addict. If the VCR didn't start whizzing soon, there would be a complete meltdown. I gave my husband "the look." He shrugged his shoulders and motioned, "The Leafs are playing." Grandma Josephine said something to Grandpa George in Yugoslavian, and Grandpa put his arm around Ronny.

Grandpa George: Do you want to watch Barney?

Ronny cuddled up to Grandpa, and the VCR started its magic bedtime ritual that signalled the evening would soon be mine. Ronny was asleep in less than ten minutes, and I was ready to move him to bed, but Grandpa said, "No, leave him." Grandpa missed half an hour of Leaf's playoff hockey to watch a purple dinosaur sing and dance just to keep his little man snuggled on his lap a little longer.

Ronny loved everything Grandpa loved. Grandpa put salt on his toast, so Ronny wanted salt on his toast. Grandpa ate Kielbasa every day for lunch, and now Ronny did too. Grandpa loved hockey, and Ronny loved hockey. They both cheered for Toronto, and the only thing Grandpa loved more than his Maple Leafs was cuddling up with Ronny to watch Barney, the big purple dinosaur.

Hockey Dad

(This is a long one, so if you're doing some bedtime reading, dog-ear this page and come back to it later—I don't want to be responsible for you being cranky tomorrow.)

A round of applause for all hockey coaches in Canada! You stepped up to the impossible dream with nothing more than blades on your feet and a big stick in your hands! There is nothing sexier to me than a grown man on centre ice surrounded by snot-nosed kids teetering on skates with looks of admiration on their faces. Every parent in the stands has NHL gleaming in their eyes, the Canadian flag in their heart, and a bit of Baileys in their coffee! Ah, the coach!

Our son, Ronny, loved hockey, and when he was old enough to walk, we did what all Canadian families do, we bought the boy a stick and the cutest little skates! We signed him up for the local recreational league, and Ron volunteered to coach. Toddlers are such a nice way to start hockey players, sharing the puck, helping each other up when they fall down and cheering no matter who scores—that's good sportsmanship, and it comes so naturally. I loved the first few years of friendly hockey, but they didn't last; my boy grew up, and his competitive nature took over. Damn hockey!

My husband has always hated a hockey game that turned into a blowout: when the score is ridiculously high for one team, painfully low for the other team, and they keep scoring even though there is no chance for the other team to make a comeback. One year, Ronny was on the dream team, and poor Ron was their coach. The offence had accurate shots, the defence was a brick wall protecting their goalie, and there were blowouts: games that ended 15–0 or 17–2. Our team was on the winning end, but Ron was no Scotty Bowman; the coach had a winning team, but he wasn't happy about it.

Ron decided when the score was more than five goals apart, both teams would make a trade. Right then and there, Ron would stop the game, skate over to the other team's bench with his strongest player, and ask for their weakest player and trade them out. It was a recreational league; the coaches were also the volunteer referees. If it was the thought that counted, Ron would have scored, but it didn't. The stronger player didn't want to score against his own team, and the weakest player just got called out as the "Weakest Player." Burn!

With the player trades not working, Ron set new rules for his team. Once the puck crossed the blue line, they had to pass the puck five times before anyone could take a shot on net. Great theory to slow down the goals, but when you have five hotshot twelve-year-old boys on the ice with the opportunity to score, they *don't* pass. They shoot, and they score. It was time for Ron to take a page out of John

Tortorella's playbook and get tough. Any player that took a shot on net before five passes were made would be benched. The kids were *pissed*, the parents were shocked, and our car rides home were silent; Ronny got benched—*a lot*.

I was getting worried that Karma either hated hockey or was partying too hard on Friday nights to make it to our Saturday morning games. It turned out she was there, but she knows hormonal boys take a little longer to understand things, so it wasn't until a couple of years later that she evened the score.

Ronny decided to move out of recreational hockey and into the Minor Hockey Association. He said it was to get more ice time and play in tournaments, but we all knew it was a problem with the coaching staff. Ron was relieved to know his coaching career was coming to an end; he was looking forward to sitting in the stands and drinking Baileys with the other parents, but that wasn't what Karma had in mind for Ron.

Our daughter, Malyn, had been on a bowling league for four years at this point. She had never bowled over 100 in a single game. If you're a bowler, you know that's terrible. If you're not a bowler, congratulations, you've lived your life out of the alley! If ever there was a sport that parents should be prescribed Valium to take while watching their kids play, it's *bowling*! Sorry, but, really—throwing a ball down a lane at pins that don't move, over and over and over... Malyn loved bowling. She was the lowest scorer in her league every single week for all four years, and she couldn't wait to go bowling every Saturday morning. Even the owners of the bowling alley were amazed at how happy Malyn was to come out every Saturday morning and bowl so badly.

Saturday mornings were divided between Ronny's hockey and Malyn's bowling. Lucky for me the rink was within walking distance to the alley, and I could do double duty if they played at the same time. The only thing Malyn didn't love about bowling was the lack of fans. Ronny often had family members come to watch his games. I couldn't invite my family to watch Malyn bowl when I could barely stand to do it myself. When Ronny moved to minor hockey, Malyn decided she would like to try recreational hockey. If she couldn't get the fans to the bowling alley, then she would take her shit show to the ice rink, and what a shit show that was!

Ron stepped back up to centre ice to coach his daughter. He was less than thrilled, but good dads are seldom thrilled dads! Malyn can't skate. I don't mean she doesn't skate well or can't do crossovers or go backwards. I mean, Malyn can't skate; in fact, she can barely stand in skates. Players would be skating all around her, and she would do her little penguin march to follow the puck, only to find out it had changed direction. Her bowling was bad, but hockey was worse. She wanted fans, but again I couldn't subject my family to this.

In the recreational league, every player had to take a turn in goal. That was my golden ticket. The week Malyn was the goalie and didn't have to skate, she only had to stand in net with two metal posts to help support her, that was the week I could invite our family. The girl wanted fanfare, and I was going to deliver. I invited everyone; I made signs: "HOLY MOLY–THAT'S OUR GOALIE." I ignored Karma's golden rule: humility.

The stands were packed (not really, but it reads well). There was a buzz in the air as the players came out on ice. It looked like the goalie was struggling in all that gear. As every player skated past her during warm-up and gave her pads a tap with their stick, she nearly fell over. Still, how bad could this be? She was in net, Ron was the coach, her teammates were kind, I made signs, invited family and had extra Baileys in my coffee—what could go wrong?

It was bad. It was like she had never seen a puck coming towards her before, and in retrospect, considering how slow she skated, she probably hadn't. He shoots, he scores; she shoots, she scores; over and over again. Malyn was a human sift in net. We were only ten minutes into the game when I quietly folded up my sign and sat on it. After the first period, Malyn needed her coach (Dad) to pull her helmet off and wipe her face—not sweat; she was crying like a baby. Her whole little face was covered in tears and snot, and she couldn't wipe them with those giant gloves. Holy Moly, that's my little girl goalie, and she wanted out of net—now! I still tear up writing this when I think of her begging her Dad to get her off the ice with all our family there to watch.

We only had one set of goalie equipment, and with no backup goalie, she had to stay in. It turned into target practice for the other team, and poor Malyn couldn't stop the puck any better than her tears. Her eyes were so puffy and full she had trouble finding the puck in her net to bring it back out in play. Some of her teammates had to go in the net to dig it out for her. Where the hell was Karma? I needed that bitch. She was there. One of Malyn's teammates offered to go in net without equipment, just so Malyn could get out. Another parent in the crowd must have felt very proud that day.

Malyn got off the ice and went right to the dressing room, where she and I tried desperately to untangle her from all those pads, straps, and ties. Eventually, she stopped crying (and so did I). We celebrated the game like any other: going out for breakfast and cheering our goalie! Malyn's hockey career only lasted one season, thank God! Again, Ron bought a big bottle of Baileys and prepared for retirement from coaching. Poor Ron, Karma wasn't done with him yet. Malyn had learned humility, but Ronny was still on a winning streak; fair is fair.

Ronny was fifteen years old and entering midget hockey. Over the years, he had various coaches. Every season had some wins and some losses but no real streaks of either—not since his winning year with that awful coach Ron in the recreational league. Midget hockey was for fifteen to seventeen-year-old kids, a very difficult age for parenting and a painful age for coaching. Ronny was staying on the house league. Only problem, the house league had no volunteer coaches, and without coaches, there would not be a midget house team. As parents, Ron and I both agreed that keeping our kids in sports and extracurricular activities kept them out of trouble. Ronny needed to stay out of trouble (an incident of drawing penises on angels a few years later confirmed this belief). House league needed a coach, and I married a smoking hot, sexy hockey coach; problem solved, but who was going to tell Ronny?

Ron signed up to coach and went to the required training. Ronny signed up for house league with a promise from his dad that he wouldn't get traded to the other team, no matter what the score was. The season started. The first game was a shut-out, 9–0. We lost. The second game was better, 6–0. Again we lost. Sadly, it went downhill from there. We couldn't win a game to save our lives. What could be worse than a team of fifteen to seventeen-year-old boys losing every game? I'll tell you. It's a bunch of cocky eight to ten-year-old boys winning every game.

Karma was a Leaf's fan after all! She was going to teach these teenagers that trying really hard could be better than winning if they did it together. It was a long, tough year for those boys, and what they lacked on the scoreboard, they gained in character. They never did win a game in that season or at any tournaments, and the head coach couldn't be prouder!

Eventually, Malyn found her superpower: music. Music is what feelings sound like, and Malyns feelings are beautiful. Malyn took vocal lessons and guitar, then a bit of piano, banjo, and self-learned the ukulele. She even took some classes on songwriting. She sings when she's happy, and she sings when she's sad. In the car, in the pool, on the lawnmower, making supper or sweeping the floor, she sings. She's done open mic nights, weddings, and YouTube videos. Singing while accompanied with her own guitar, she shines. People ask us from which side of the family she got her talent from, and I answer honestly: it wasn't inherited from either of us; that's all Malyn.

After a dozen years of coaching in two different leagues, Ron finally got to taste Baileys in his coffee. Ah—the coach could finally retire.

From Accounting to Aqua Fit?!

My high school career improved after dropping phys ed, but I was never particularly strong in any subject until I took accounting. Ah, accounting, I loved it! You started with two item journal entries, then went from ledger accounts to trial balance all the way to income statement or balance sheet. These seemingly inconsequential items were all put together to tell a story about the time, energy, and overall potential a business had. It was true storytelling at its best. All the rules made sense, and they never changed. It was simple—follow the rules and balance, and you get to keep playing. If you don't follow the rules, you don't balance, back to the start. Every hormonal teenager should really sink their teeth into a good accounting course to make sense of the world. (It didn't work for my kids, but that's another story.)

After high school, I took a three-year business program with a major in accounting. College itself was a bit of a shock, but I *loved* my program. I thrived in accounting, auditing, and taxation; I tolerated marketing, music, and psych—yes, you guessed it, I was one of the cool kids! I graduated on the Dean's list. It was the first time in my life that I could really kick ass at something. I was ready to debit my way into a great job and credit my way to the top of it!

I worked in accounting for twenty-five years with small and medium-sized companies. I was freelanced to smaller places that needed someone to do the books but were not big enough to have a full or even part-time position for me. I had a variety of clients that I went to work for or that brought their records to me. I really liked my job, and I was good at it. I can't share any of my accounting stories—there is this thing called "client confidentiality." If you break it, you go to hell where nothing balances, columns do not line up, and the addition is all wrong. It's hell, and I won't go. No accounting stories.

In my mid-forties I still liked my job, but I wasn't excited about it anymore. I had been researching the certification processes for teaching aqua fit and financially mapped out how many classes I would need to teach to justify quitting my job and taking the aqua fit plunge. From a financial view, I should keep my job, but money isn't everything, and who knows, maybe this aqua fit thing could really take off. I gave my notice with the promise that I would stay until they found someone to replace me. Ten months later was my last day (yes, it would have been quicker and possibly less painful to have a baby), but I left on good terms and still consider them all friends.

For twenty-five years, I sat behind a desk saying, "No, that is not in the budget. No, that is not deductible. No, that won't pass an audit." To a job that I stood up and yelled, "Chin in, shoulders back, tall spine, and *smile!*" I had gone over the deep end, mind, body and spirit, and to celebrate how crazy it all was, that's what I named my new business: Over The Deep End. Yes, of course, Off The Deep End would have been more accurate, but accuracy is for accounting; that was my past, my future was going to unfold the way I wrote it!

Watch What You Eat!

If you're expecting to read about the secret of weight loss and increased energy, here it is: there is *no secret*. You want to lose some extra pounds and feel better? Eat your damn vegetables. That's it. Honestly, don't like veggies? Grow up and eat your damn vegetables!

Now then, some funny Fischtner food stories…

I do most of the cooking in our house, but when the kids were small, my husband Ron would make Sunday big breakfast: bacon and eggs, or pancakes and sausage, toast, hashbrowns—the works! Ron has never been good in the kitchen; he tries (rarely and half-heartedly), but we all have our strengths, and his aren't in the culinary arts. One Sunday, he was up to his elbows in our "big breakfast," and he had finished frying the bacon and drained the fat into a coffee cup to cool. While buttering the toast and calling us all in to eat, he took a swig from his coffee. While paying no attention to which coffee cup he grabbed, he took a big gulp of warm gooey *bacon fat*! Breakfast got cold while the kids and I laughed, and poor Ron brushed his teeth and rinsed his mouth like a maniac. Watch what you eat!

My daughter Malyn loves pancakes. She is a self-proclaimed pancake whore (for those of you that don't know what that is, it's anyone who can eat half their body weight in pancakes). She would have been eight or nine years old when we were on vacation and having breakfast in a restaurant a little fancier than she was used to. Of course, she ordered the pancakes. I thought she was going to break into song when they arrived, and she found them topped with what she thought was a dollop of vanilla ice cream. She wasn't about to let that ice cream melt on her hot pancakes while I tried to explain that it wasn't ice cream. She scooped it up in one huge spoonful and popped all that whipped *butter* in her mouth in one giant bite! What can I say? The apple doesn't fall far from the tree. Watch what you eat!

I was raised in a house where you ate what was on your plate at the kitchen table every night at 6:00 p.m. Didn't like it?—didn't matter. Didn't want it?—no one asked you. Other plans?—no such thing. My husband was raised in a house where you ate whatever you wanted, whenever you wanted, and in whatever room you wanted. We both had some compromising to do. I won on eating at the table at 5:30 daily. He won on no fighting at the table if the kids didn't like the meal.

For the first three years of my young son's life, my husband would pop up from the table to make Ronny his requested toast and jam. He did this for breakfast, lunch and, yes, dinner—there were no arguments. Ronny wanted toast, and Daddy made toast. Now, of course, every person reading this is asking themselves, "really?" Yes, really, and it had to end. We started insisting he eat what I made (covered in cheese and sometimes jam). He was getting better, but there were arguments; he was a very fussy eater.

When Ronny was six years old, I decided it was time for Ronny to eat mild Italian sausage, and it would be done in my family style: at the table, and you don't get off the table until your plate is clean. He started with ten bite-size pieces of sausage. He negotiated it down to four (I was tired, and it was getting late; I caved). There he sat with the sausage on his plate and him crying, not just a few tears and some whining, it was a soul-breaking flood of mournful crying. I couldn't take it, so I left the room. Ron wasn't far behind me. We agreed that this was going badly, but as good, responsible parents, we had to follow through and be consistent with what we said.

I don't know which of us came up with this plan, so let's assume it was Ron…

We had a dog named Cuddles (who made puddles, but that is another story). She was a lovable little poodle. Cuddles had a dog dish with kibble in it, but that was just to lead our guests to believe that she ate dog food. Cuddles lived on table scraps. We all fed her, and we fed her well. Ron and I decided that if we stayed hidden in the bedroom and sent Cuddles out to "sit" with Ronny at the table, surely Ronny would feed the dreaded sausage to Cuddles and our nightmare of good parenting would end for the evening. We sent Cuddles out. The crying continued. We explained to Ronny that we would stay in the bedroom with the door closed. The crying continued. We went out and asked, "Did you feed Cuddles your sausage?" (in case he hadn't thought of it). The crying continued. Ronny was a smart kid, but sadly for Ron and me, he was also honest. The sausage was cold and dry, Ronny's eyes were swollen and sore, and Ron and I had learned the lesson: choose your battles!

Cuddles enjoyed the sausage, I praised Ronny for his honesty, and Ron made toast and jam.

Say What You Mean and Mean What You Say

I'm forever telling Ron and our kids, say what you mean *and* mean what you say. If you say you will be ready in twenty minutes, then *be ready* in twenty minutes. Don't say one thing and do something else altogether. It's simple and easy to follow unless what you say is *really* not what you mean...

Ron rarely gets rattled if little things go wrong. He just rolls with the punches—unless Tim Horton's doesn't have sour cream for his bagels, then he loses his shit. Ron went into Tim's to get us coffee and bagels. He likes cream cheese on his bagel, and that is what he meant to ask for, but what he said was sour cream. He ordered his bagel with sour cream, and the thirteen-year-old cashier said, "sour cream?"

"Ya, sour cream," Ron said. Again the cashier hesitated then said, "I don't think we have sour cream."

These young kids today don't even know what sour cream is, Ron thought. "Yes you do. They put sour cream on bagels all the time."

Ron wanted his bagel and sour cream, and this kid needed to find some!

The kid went to the sandwich-making station and asked, "Do we have any sour cream?"

The answer was a curt, "No, we don't have sour cream," followed by an unspoken but implied, *you idiot!*

The poor kid had to go back to Ron and say, "Sorry, we don't have sour cream here."

Ron came back to the car where I was waiting and repeated to me his plight for sour cream. He was outraged that the kid didn't seem to even know what sour cream was and that they didn't actually have any?!

Ron: Can you believe that? What kind of Tim Horton's doesn't have sour cream for their bagels?

Me: I've heard cream cheese is good on bagels too, maybe try that next time?

Say what you mean and mean what you say.

We were driving Malyn and her cousin Steven home from high school when a car pulled out in front of us and totally cut us off. Ron was driving, and I was in the passenger seat. My family will tell you I have a road rage issue; that's not true! I have rude rage issues. There is a difference. Anyone can make a mistake while driving, but when you make eye contact with another driver and then cut them off, that's rude! Ron didn't so much as flinch at the driver that cut us off, which only pissed me off even more. What I meant to say was, If I were driving, I'd give her the finger and honk my horn too! But what I actually said was, "If I were driving, I'd give her the horn and finger her too!" Yeah, that's not what I meant at all. With two teenagers in the back seat,

I said a silent prayer that no one had heard me. The quiet giggles erupted into raging laughter; they heard me. For years whenever a driver would irritate me, Malyn would ask, "What do you think, Mom, should you finger her too?"

Say what you mean, and mean what you say.

Go to Your Room While I Do Your Homework!

I was nervous when my kids started high school (probably a little PTSD from my own high school days). I was worried they wouldn't do well or would hang out with the wrong crowd. I always volunteered in their elementary school, so I had my finger on the pulse of what was going on there. High school didn't have a healthy snack program or scrapbook club for me to volunteer at; I was going to have to sit on the sidelines for this shit show.

Ronny got through with passing grades while exerting as little effort as possible. His locker was a pigsty, and some of his teachers didn't appreciate his sense of humour. The most trouble he got into was when he drew penises on the Christmas angels that decorated the hallways. Proud moment for us indeed, but if that's the worst he did, then give my boy a Sharpie and an angel! Yeah, team Fischtner. One down, one to go.

Malyn was the opposite; good grades meant everything to her. She would finish assignments long before their due date just to make sure she always had time to study for possible pop quizzes. All this academic excellence was going to come to a grinding halt in Grade 11 when she decided to take accounting.

In elementary school, it was expected for parents to help with homework; in high school, I knew my help wouldn't be encouraged, but how could I not help her? She was struggling right from the get-go. I couldn't let her fail in a subject that I made a career of. She just needed a little tutoring and gentle encouragement. Together, we would figure things out.

Oh, my god, there must have been a mix-up in the hospital. There is no way any child of mine could be this dense in basic bookkeeping. Seriously, she didn't have a clue. I would explain calmly, and then again, a little louder so she could hear me, and finally again with some theatrics to really drive it home for her—and still, nothing!

The rule in our house was that homework had to be done before dinner so I wouldn't have to yell on a full stomach. It was dinner time, and my thick-headed little girl couldn't debit or credit her way out of a wet paper bag. Ron was coming in for dinner just as I yelled, "Go to your room while I do your homework, and don't come out until I'm done!" You couldn't slap the smile off that girl's face while she went to her room.

It was a very long semester for both of us, and despite Malyn getting a final grade of ninety-two percent in accounting, she still knows virtually nothing about bookkeeping!

Take Your Shot at a Great Party

When the kids were young, I threw a lot of theme parties for their friends and cousins. For March Break, we had Fear Factor Parties. For New Year's Eve, we had parties at the cabin with skating on the pond, but it was for the birthday parties that I pulled out all the stops.

Malyn's birthday is July 29th, but it is celebrated (mostly by her) *all* month. Malyn loves her birthday and was in shock when I explained her nineteenth would be the last year that I would throw her a themed party. She couldn't understand why the tradition had to end in her twenties. This was the same girl that still believed in Santa Claus in Grade 8. When I told her the truth, that there is a spirit of Christmas, just not a Santa Claus, she was devastated. Her first question was, "What about the Easter Bunny? He's real, right?" That was a rough day for poor Malyn. She always had great birthday parties; she had a detective party, a princess party, and a spy games party. For her sixteenth, she had an Amazing Race party all through Strathroy. For her nineteenth, it was a scavenger hunt to find the clues in the backyards of people in our aqua fit family. The party girl and all her friends loved those parties; my son, on the other hand…

Ronny was more subdued about his birthdays. I did theme parties for him too, but he always wanted something a little more low-key. For his tenth birthday, we did a cap gun party in the bush. It was by far his favourite party. His friends loved it too, even if some of the parents thought we were as redneck as they get. For his nineteenth birthday and final party, I thought we could relive his tenth. We hired someone to come to the bush, set up decoys, and organize teams for a paintball party. It was a surprise for Ronny; we invited his friends, rented guns for everyone, and loaded up on paintballs. They spent all afternoon shooting in the bush and then got to what every nineteenth birthday is about, drinking! I brought them food to absorb all the liquor and asked Ronny if I could take just one shot. I wanted to take a shot at Ronny, and with all his friends cheering him on, my big little boy couldn't say no.

First of all, I hate guns—I am truly terrified of them. Growing up on a farm, I experienced guns as part of our landscape, guns were a tool to my Dad's deadstock business. To keep us kids safe, my parents put the fear of God into us about guns. Up to the age of fourteen, I was convinced if you looked too closely at a gun, it could fire at you. I don't know why I wanted to shoot Ronny so badly, but there was a burning desire in me to shoot that boy.

I needed a lesson on how to hold the gun (they are heavy!) and then how to aim the gun (keep one eye open), and finally, how to fire the gun (pull that trigger). Through all this, Ronny was standing in wait. His friends were half-drunk and enjoying the show. It was time for Ronny to face the firing squad: his mama. He stood far enough away that I couldn't hurt him too badly, but close enough that I wouldn't miss. He had his back to me; I was afraid if I had to look him in those puppy dog eyes, I wouldn't go through with it.

If you've ever been in a dunk tank, where they throw balls at an arm to drop the seat and plunge you into a barrel of cold water, you know that waiting for that ball to connect to the arm is much worse than the actual plunge into cold water. Waiting to be shot in the back is much the same.

Ronny was ready, his friends were ready, and I wanted to savour the moment and needed some last-minute tips from the expert.

Me: So, should I go a little high or a little low on this shot?

The pro pointed where I needed to be.

Ronny: Come on, Mom, take the shot.

Me: Will it hurt you, like leave a bruise or anything?

Ronny: It's fine, Mom, just take the shot.

Me: How many times do you think I've asked you to clean your room?

His friends were loving this; of course, they had mothers and filthy bedrooms too.

Ronny: I don't know, Mom, but you're only getting *one* shot, so how about you just take it already?

Me: I only get one shot, but how many times do you think I've asked you to brush your teeth?

Ronny was starting to lose his shit here. He had been standing in front of my gun for a long time.

Ronny: Just shoot me already, Mom. Please—just shoot me now!

I know you're reading this and thinking, *She won't do it. How could a loving mother shoot her son in the back?* Well, I'll tell you how. Hold the gun at your shoulder, aim with one eye open, and pull the damn trigger!

Now you're probably thinking that I'm going to write about how bad I felt after shooting the poor boy on his birthday in front of all his friends. Wrong again! It was wonderful. It felt great! I don't know how long I wanted to do that but, it was awesome. Even three days later, when his bruise had turned to that ugly purple colour, I still marvelled at how good it felt.

Trust me on this, if you have a teenage son and the opportunity to shoot him in the back with a paintball, take the shot. It's more therapeutic than counselling, more calming than yoga, and more fun than a night out with the girls. Take the shot, my friend. You won't regret it.

Don't Wear Dresses on Windy Days

I love dresses! I love dresses for summer, spring, fall, and yes, I have winter dresses too. My love for dresses was born out of my aversion to shopping. Tops and bottoms had to match, tucked or untucked. Belt, socks, shoes, accessories— who has time for all that? Buy a dress, slip it over your head, and slide into your sandals; good to go!

Summer dresses are my favourite, and I wear each and every dress I own at least once every season. My mother was a very organized woman, and she taught me that if you didn't wear something in your closet for one full year, you need to give it away. I couldn't give away any of my lovely dresses, but the truth was, a couple of them were ready to make a run for it themselves.

I was wearing a dress from my younger days. By that, I mean low cut, spaghetti straps, light and bouncy, and of course, above the knees. I classed it up with a wide stretch belt with a big shiny buckle. You're probably thinking, "*Date night?*" Nope, Tuesday.

Malyn and I had to do some errands in town that afternoon. One of our stops was to pick up a repaired tire. As it happens, the manager of the tire shop is one of Malyn's best friends' dad. Mark is a gentleman, and of course, he carried the tire out to our car for us. After the tire was loaded, we were talking about the girls and their upcoming plans. I noticed Malyn, who was sitting in the car, signalling me of a wardrobe malfunction. Sure enough, my big stretchy belt had tried to eat the itty-bitty top half of my dress! I was desperately trying to cover my top half up when a wind came up behind me and completely lifted the lower half of my dress. Of course, this was the day I just had to wear my cheetah print underwear! I was pulling my top up, my bottom down, the wind kept blowing, and Mark kept talking. *Shit!*

I got back in the car thinking maybe it wasn't that bad. You know how sometimes you think everyone sees you do something stupid and it turns out no one even noticed? I hadn't even closed my car door when Malyn said, "Cheetah print? *Really?* You wore cheetah print underwear under *that* dress?"

OK, so she saw it. That doesn't mean Mark did, except, ya, he did too.

It is an ongoing joke that Mark owes me dinner now that he's seen me half-naked. Lucky for me, his wife laughs at the jokes as hard as my husband does! And just to set the record straight for Mark and everyone else in the tire shop, I threw that stupid dress out!

Life Bridge

We've got through some ups and downs, a few laughs and a few tears; now you know how it feels to be a Leaf's fan. Well, fans, I promise you there is a game-changer coming in 2010!

You've met my team and know their talent (none, basically), and in the next few chapters, you will witness me dropping the gloves and fighting more than once (sadly with my own teammates). Personally, I move from being a strong defensive player to centre-ice! After years of rumours, there is finally going to be a league expansion in a new city known as Funkytown.

Crossing this bridge takes you to a very exciting time with lots of laughs. This is the stuff that makes a true Leaf's fan a lifelong Leaf's fan. Keep your stick on the ice—the puck is about to drop!

Successful Women Build Foundations from the Stones Others Have Thrown

Although we had an outdoor pool, I wanted an indoor pool. I suffered from seasonal affective disorder, also known as SAD, and, in short, it makes you feel sad. In the winter, there just isn't enough vitamin D from the sun, and for some of us, it really makes a mess of our emotions. There were several winters that I needed anti-depressants to make it to spring. Winter was my least favourite season, but I tried to make peace with it. I went cross country skiing, skating, tobogganing, and even snowmobiling (or shit-mobiling as I like to call it!). My husband hates to fly, and I hate boats, so winter escapes south weren't an option for us. Winter is a very long season in Canada, and for some of us, hockey and Canadian Club just aren't enough to pull us through it!

Every year when the outdoor pool was winterized and covered, I would cry. Covering the pool meant winter was coming, and winter made me sad. I always thought, if I had a pool that never got winterized, I would always have a warm, sunny place of refuge from the cold, harsh snow. If you read that sentence and thought, "*Wow, this chick is bat shit crazy,*" then you know exactly how my husband felt.

For seven long years, we "discussed" building an indoor pool. Some of our "discussions" ended with slamming doors or name-calling, and yes, there was some colourful language used. It was a big endeavour, and once you got started, you couldn't turn back. There just aren't a lot of decorating options that work around a 700-square-foot hole that is nine feet deep. Ron researched (stalled) for a long time. The first plan was to cover the existing pool we had, but you can't share the air between your house and your pool. The humidity from the pool would make your whole house humid and risk mould on drywall and window sills. We scrapped those blueprints (yes, we actually had blueprints done). Then we came up with a brilliant idea of a tunnel between our house and pool and had that drawn up in a blueprint. It was ridiculous. No question—that was stupid.

Ron felt like a hero. He tried every which way; it just wouldn't work for our pool. Too bad, so sad. Poor Ron, even he would forget from time to time that I am bat shit crazy. I decided, if we couldn't cover the pool we had, then we needed to build another pool.

This indoor pool was turning into a bad case of untreated herpes for Ron; it wasn't going away, and it was getting worse! Our "discussions" got even more colourful, and eventually, when I had exhausted everything else, I went below the belt. No, I'm not talking about sex! Get your head out of the gutter; my kids are going to read this book! The tears were coming, and there was no stopping them once the flood gate was released. Ron can ignore a lot of my jibber, but when I cry, his world stops spinning.

After seven years, the shit got real! First, new blueprints! Neither of us wanted to call the architect after ditching the first two blueprints, but he just laughed and asked, "Are you sure this time, like *really* sure this time?" Next, dig the pool. That's exciting. There is no turning back once that excavator takes a few big bites.

I was home the first day they started, and I remember hearing the ear-splitting clunk of metal hitting cement. I didn't know much about moving earth, but I knew that didn't sound good.

My parents gave us three acres of land and helped us build our house. It was my dad's idea to build it on an angle, and I'm so thankful we took his advice. Building the house as we did left room for us to build the body shop and the pool, Karma or my dad? Sometimes they worked together on bigger projects. My dad staked out where our house would go. There was a cement silo that was buried at the back of the property that we had to stay away from when designing the house. Guess where I decided to build the pool? Yup, that cement silo that my dad told me to stay away from. I can see him looking down at me shaking his head, rubbing his chin, and saying, "Couldn't listen to the old man, huh?" I listened, dad; problem was, I forgot.

Again, poor Ron thought he won a get out of jail free card; if we couldn't put the new pool there, then we couldn't put it anywhere. No pool, but hey, he *really* tried! I didn't invest seven years into this only to have a cement silo stop me. We had to dig it up and move it or break it into smaller pieces that we could work on top of. This was happening one way or another, Ron. Call another excavator. I had four years of watching Mighty Machines with my son; I knew there was another machine for that mighty job. Let's get it!

February 2010, the pool was filled, the building done, and the propane tanks filled! A lot of people thought we were crazy, and we were, but it was the good kind of crazy. I had always imagined the finished product to look like an outdoor room that was indoors, and that is exactly what it was. There are high ceilings with lots of windows to let in my beloved sun. Snow squalls, ice pellets, wind chill, bring it on. I wasn't sad anymore!

Riding Noodles May Cause Chafing

After the pool was built, we hosted family gatherings, and the kids had friends over all the time. Every Sunday, we would lie in our floaters and watch a movie from the pool. Malyn had a little side business called "Swim with Malyn" on Saturday mornings. She would have three or four little ones come for a half-day of swimming, snacks, games, and basic babysitting in a pool.

The second winter we had the pool, I got an email from a friend asking if she could rent it two evenings a week for aqua fit classes with her friends. I didn't want to rent the pool out, and I didn't want to share it more than once a week, but I liked the idea of aqua fit classes. We agreed to one night a week, and instead of rent, they would make a donation to a charity of my choice (Down Syndrome). I could attend the class, and it would be taught by her friend, Judy McNeill. There were anywhere from three to eight ladies each week that came to those first classes. We were all in different ages and stages of life, different careers, different ideals but the same love of water and need to connect on a personal level.

Back then, we didn't have belts or tethers, or dumbbells and paddles; all we had was pool noodles. We all liked doing deep water aqua fit, but an hour of treading water without a floatation belt was a stretch. To keep us afloat, we each straddled a pool noodle; it kept us up and allowed our arms and legs to keep doing the moves as Judy instructed.

Week after week we rode those noodles. Now most of you have probably never ridden a pool noodle for an hour a week. Those noodles do break down and get rough, and let's face it, ladies, our inner thighs have very sensitive skin. Chafing was becoming a very delicate problem for all of us.

I was still at my accounting job, and two of the ladies from the office had joined our aqua fit class. For the staff Christmas party that year, we did a Secret Santa gift exchange. Everyone had to open their gift from an anonymous Santa in front of everyone. I will never forget the bright red face of my co-worker when she opened her gift: a bottle of baby powder. The three of us were the only ones that knew what it was for, which left everyone else making some wild guesses.

It was unanimously agreed, we all needed some baby powder and buoyancy belts. The first waves of Over The Deep End had rippled. The following year, I decided to leave my accounting career and start my own business at the pool: deepwater adult aqua fit classes. I had no competition in a town that had no indoor pool. Of course, I also had no customers, no instructors, no equipment, and no training. I had totally and completely gone Over The Deep End.

Funkytown

The pool was built, I had left my job in accounting, and for the first time in over thirty years, I was unemployed. I was registered for CALA (Canadian Aquafitness Leaders Alliance) certification courses, but I had two months of downtime before I could start teaching aqua fit. It was time to get the pool ready for business and my body in shape to start teaching.

I needed to build change rooms, put in a bathroom, add a sand filter, buy aqua fit equipment, and a sound system. I was spending a lot of money in a building that I had already spent a small fortune on, and I just quit my job. Ouch.

Ron and the kids were behind me every step of the way, and by that, I mean, way behind me. I had visions of full classes and women getting into shape, all thanks to me and my pool—it was aqua-extraordinaire, and I was the Queen of Chlorine. Ron and the kids knew that when things didn't go as I planned, I fell and fell hard. They wanted to keep me grounded and realistic. Every new business takes time to grow, and they were happy to give me all the time I needed. Their only worry was living with me during that time; patience is a virtue, and, as you can read in this book, I'm not a virtuous woman.

I wanted to build four change stalls; each stall separate from the other to provide complete privacy. Ron thought I was nuts to want four change rooms.

Ron: Do you really think you will ever have four people here for classes at the same time?

Me: Hell no, I expect there to be eight people here for each class, and they can take turns using the four change stalls before and after class. This way, there won't be too much downtime between each class starting and finishing.

Sadly, this explanation didn't make him feel any better. What he thought didn't matter; I knew who to call to get it built, and he had no problem working for a woman who knew what she wanted, even if her husband questioned her sanity.

Next, my body needed a serious tune-up. I had become a gym enthusiast, but that didn't erase the forty hours a week I spent sitting on my ass behind a desk for twenty-five years. I needed to move and groove; it was time for Dance Dance Revolution! I had spent hours applauding my kids on the air guitar, air drums, and vocals playing Rock Band on the Wii (hey, it was a step up from bowling). It was my turn for centre stage.

I played Dance Dance Revolution for hours every day. I was awesome. From beginner to advanced to expert, I had gone to Funkytown. No, literally, that was my song, "Funkytown." I spent every day getting better at that one song. Yes, there were lots of other songs, but my song was

"Funkytown," and if you keep doing the same song over and over, you get really good at it.

It was time for a Dance Off! Malyn was in Grade 7, and as soon as she got off the bus, I challenged her to a dance competition, one song only: "Funkytown." I nailed it. I would slay her every day. It got boring. I was so good, and she wasn't getting any better—time to invite her friends over. Come on, girls, let's play Dance Dance Revolution. Yes, I am the coolest mom ever! I nailed it. Over and over, I would dance those little girls into oblivion.

Those two months flew by, and before I knew it, I was ready to move to a town that was right for me. A town that would keep me moving and grooving with energy. I had talked about it, talked about moving on. It was time to go to Funkytown.

God Bless the Guinea Pigs

If you want to learn something, read about it. If you want to understand something, research it. If you want to master something, teach it.

It was time to teach. I had taken my CALA courses, and the pool was ready and waiting with all those change rooms! I needed volunteers to take classes. I offered classes free of charge to friends and family; all they had to do was commit to one class a week for four weeks and answer a short survey after the first and the last class.

My sister Margaret was at my very first class. I was nervous as a nun in a whore house. Sorry for the visual, but really, I was *that* nervous. After that first class, Margaret came to me and said, "You look euphoric." She was right. I felt *euphoric*. I didn't just step out of my comfort zone; I sprinted out of it naked! Looking back now, it was probably the worst class I had taught in terms of muscle groups and choreographing, but I was engaged with the group, and they were energized by my enthusiasm. I still had a lot to learn and mistakes yet to make but going Over The Deep End was where I belonged, and this was way better than beating little girls at Dance Dance Revolution. Goodbye Funkytown, I've moved on.

Each week I taught the classes, and I became a little more confident. I had a long way to go, but I had the right group of women to help me get there. Many of the women in those guinea pig classes are still in classes with me now, and one day I'll stop calling them guinea pigs, but not yet.

Sherrie was one of my first and favourite guinea pigs. She had just quit smoking. A big round of applause for everyone that wrestled that monkey off their back! She had a smile for everyone who crossed her path and a gentle easiness about her. She was so inquisitive that we call her Barbara Walters. With her attention on everyone else, you would be hard-pressed to find out that she suffers from MS.

Sherrie became the one-woman Welcome Wagon representative for Over The Deep End. She did registration for me on the first week of every new session. She would orientate new customers and welcome back the regulars. Registration was the easy part of her job; listening to my neurotic ramblings when we first started and always being a soft place for Malyn to land was the tougher part.

I think COVID hit Sherrie much harder than MS did. Sherrie is a hugger, and I'm not talking birthday hugs or condolences hugs. I'm talking "I haven't seen you since yesterday" hugs. Wet bathing suit hugs and see you tomorrow hugs. Six feet distancing? Sherrie had to grow longer arms. Some people need to stay busy, some need to meditate, and some need to medicate. Sherrie needs to hug.

At the essence of every hug is the feeling of support, someone there to hold you in case you fall. Malyn was falling. She was always nervous as a child, and a worldwide pandemic can shake the strongest foundation. During the pandemic, Sherrie was her go-to; Malyn would spend hours on the phone with Sherrie unloading her feelings, falling, and being caught. When her head was spinning, and I was tough loving her, Sherrie was giving her hugs. It takes a village, and I just can't imagine living in a village without Sherrie.

Fifty Shades of Fitness

The first year of classes, we had no tethers for our participants. This meant everyone was floating around with their buoyancy belt but couldn't hold their spot in the water. Turbulence caused havoc for the hardest working participants. The harder they worked, the more turbulence they caused, and that would pull other participants in towards them. We would have eight people in the pool, and six of them would be desperately trying to push away from the strongest one in the middle. I'm not going to lie; from up on deck, it was hilarious to watch. The harder they worked to get away, the more they were pulled in.

Judy and I were at a CALA conference where we were introduced to water running. We were at a city pool in Mississauga, where they put up the lane ropes and gave each of us a tether that would attach to our belt on one end and to the rope with the other end. The tethers were simple bungee cords with plastic hooks on either end. In the water, we all had to tether each other to the rope, as they were too short for us to hook ourselves. There was a moment for me, after I was tethered, that I looked down into the twenty feet of deep water and realized I was tied to a rope that I couldn't get off myself. I had to fight back a panic attack that wanted to steal the show.

We loved that class; water running was cardio and muscle and exactly what we wanted to teach at our pool. We needed those damn tethers. With my best friend Karma and my pool sista Judy we made a plan to sidetrack the group after class and make our way back to the equipment room. We only needed one tether to figure out how to rig it up at our pool. The plan was for Judy to smuggle it into her towel while I stood watch at the door and ran interference on route back to the locker room. We were high on the class and the crime! It is laughable now; we stole a one-foot bungee cord with a plastic hook, but we both were downright giddy about our crime spree. This new career was bringing out a darker side in both of us!

Finding those tethers for our pool was more difficult than we thought. I wanted tethers that they could attach and take off themselves and that would hold up in saltwater. After many tries and fails, we found titanium carabiners that held up in saltwater and had a quick release for safety. We were ready to tie up our ladies!

Now we needed some equipment; we had dumbbells, but not everyone could use them. We wanted paddles. We ordered finger paddles that attached easily to hands and covered a lot of surface area to really intensify the upper body workout. If you don't know the difference between your triceps and your biceps, you will after using those—the bicep is the one that hurts!

We had belts that we strapped as tightly as we could around their waists, we had tethers to tie them to the wall, and we had paddles to make them hurt! This all came together while the book *Fifty Shades of Grey* was becoming a best seller! The jokes were endless! If you have read the book, you know what I'm talking about, and if you haven't read it, you should!

Epoxy Lips

When I decided to start teaching aqua fit, the first course I took for certification was in Ottawa for a course in water yoga. I was so excited. I love Ottawa. If you haven't been, *go*! Go in the winter and see Winterlude; if you're Canadian, it is a must, and if you're not Canadian, you will want to apply for citizenship!

I was scared and excited to start a new career and meet my new village! I had fully prepared my body, mind, and soul for this course by taking five hours of land yoga classes two weeks prior (if you're a yogi, you will know that is like trimming your own bangs and then calling yourself a hairdresser—bullshit).

The first night, everyone had to stand up and introduce themselves by sharing how long they've taught aqua fit and or yoga and what they like best about each. The first lady stood and said she had taught aqua fit for twenty-plus years and yoga for eight years; she liked both equally. The next lady stood and shared that she was a personal trainer full-time and taught both aqua fit and yoga part-time and liked helping people reach their fitness potential. Next was a lady that had done her yoga teacher training in India and her aqua fit training in New Zealand and had made a career teaching both for more than twenty-five years. It went on and on like that; they all had years of experience in both aqua fit and yoga. They all had a connection to the fitness industry, and through that, they had a connection to each other. My anxiety grew as my turn got closer. What the hell was I going to say, "I've been working in accounting for the last twenty-five years, and I've never taught a single class of aqua fit or yoga. I'm going through an early mid-life crisis and decided a career change would be better than a new car or a divorce, so here I am?" I can't tell a lie to save my life, so that is exactly what I said. There was a moment of silence while everyone gazed upon the waterless mermaid, and then I was saved; the instructor welcomed me and applauded my courage.

That night, I went back to the hotel where my husband and kids were excited to hear about my new adventure. I told them it was great, there was a lot to learn, and I was tired. Then I went to take a tub. I sat in that tub crying and trying to find a way to tell my family, "I don't want to go back tomorrow. I made a mistake—this isn't my village." I could either spend the weekend with people I didn't fit in with and likely fail the course or set the example of quitting without really trying for my young and impressionable kids to watch and learn from.

I made a strong drink, drank it fast, went to bed, got up in the morning, and went back to school. It was a tough course for me. The instructor made an effort to include me, and by the end of the weekend, I made some friends and had a newfound respect for yoga, both on land and in water.

To complete the course and finish the certification, I needed to do a practical assessment. The assessor lived in British Columbia, so I was able to videotape a class that I would teach at my own pool and send it to him for marking. I had a group of women that had been taking water yoga with me; they agreed to have me videotape a class with them for my practical.

Now a word about my water yoga class. If you are imagining a quiet, subdued group of ladies softly chanting "Om" together, you are very, very wrong. This is a group of women that laugh hysterically while another has fallen off their noodle swing, plunged underwater, and is gasping for air (Om indeed!). This is a group of women that have a preference for the hard noodles between their legs rather than the semi-soft squishy ones. This is a group of ladies that have taken a pact: "What happens at water yoga class stays at water yoga class." If you have never been to a yoga class that is riddled with talking, laughing, and the occasional F-bomb, you haven't been to my yoga class. It's not your typical yoga class, I'm not your typical yoga teacher, and every week we laugh, share, and hold some kick-ass yoga poses.

I was preparing for the video and needed my class to "get their shit together." They were cracking jokes and threatened to wear matching bathing suits and bathing caps on video day. Can you imagine grown women in matching glittery bathing caps? Sadly, I could. I tried to explain that they would have to be quiet for the video, that I had to appear somewhat "professional." Well, this brought on a fresh round of jokes and laughter. It was at this point that I threatened to glue all their lips shut with epoxy. Epoxy is an industrial adhesive that can bond almost anything. I wouldn't actually do that, but it did get their attention.

The day came to do my video; I was nervous—it was my first practical. I got everyone in place, we had a few laughs, ran through the flow of things, and then Malyn pressed record, and the room went deadly quiet. I thought, *OK, they are nervous too; once I get started, we will all loosen up…or not*. I was leading the class as planned and not a sound from the women. At one point, I even made a joke to the camera about how quiet they were in hopes they would give a little laugh… Nope. Thirty-five minutes of nothing but my voice and sixteen eyes monitoring my every move. Never in my life has a class been so quiet. Apparently, just the threat of epoxy was strong enough to seal their lips.

How did I do on the practical, you ask? I failed the first time around, but that's another story…

Diagnosing EFT

CALA (Canadian Aquafitness Leaders Alliance) has an annual Aqua Fit conference. The first conference I attended was the best! Judy McNeill and I went together, and we were blown away by the energy of the group. We were both still in the honeymoon stage of our aqua fit careers and were thrilled to find people as excited about aqua fit as we were. These conferences were held in Toronto and attracted aqua fit instructors from Windsor to Oshawa. Most of the instructors worked at big city pools; there were very few instructors from private pools. They had large drop-in classes that meant being prepared to lead a class with no idea of the fitness levels of their participants. Judy and I had the luxury of teaching small groups that registered for a specific style of class. We were a little bit spoiled compared to this group.

We attended workshops in the water and on land. We learned what was trending in the fitness industry and what new equipment was coming to aqua fit. Workshops were great, but the real education always happened in the locker rooms. After a pool session, there would be twenty-five to seventy-five women showering and changing to get to the next workshop. It was mayhem: not enough showers, dressing rooms, or lockers, and naked women everywhere! Everyone was charged up from the workshop, and in the locker room, everyone talked about their classes affectionately with pride and with some laugh-out-loud honesty.

We learned about one pool at which an aqua fit class had circulated a petition to have no music played at their class. Another class had requested that management interview new people to join their class to make sure newcomers would fit in. It was here that we first learned of a common condition called EFT. Many instructors had participants that suffered from it. It affected men and women alike and at all ages. The symptoms varied with each person. The only similarity, it seemed, was that everyone who suffered from EFT had several symptoms; there was never just one but many, many symptoms. Everyone seemed to know someone with EFT, while Judy and I didn't even know what EFT was! Finally, Judy asked one of our buck-naked colleagues, what exactly is EFT? Her eyes went as big as her nipples (like saucers)! "You don't know what EFT is?!"

One of my very first customers suffered from EFT; I just didn't know it at the time. She registered for a class explaining she used to swim all the time. By "used to," I found out she meant forty years ago. She assured me she had no fear of deep water. Yes, some health issues, but she would explain that later at the pool.

When she came to her first class, she couldn't keep her bottom down. I tried to explain she needed to use her core.

Customer: My left ankle is fused, and I had my right hip replaced. It's not my core; it's this damn buoyancy belt.

She insisted that she take it off. With the belt off, she still had the same problem, but now she was sinking and gasping. I explained she had to do small breaststrokes to stay afloat without the belt.

Customer: I have a frozen shoulder and can't do the stupid breaststroke that you are going on about.

I gave her a noodle to hold with her hands that would help leverage her bottom down while keeping her head above water.

Customer: This noodle is too hard to keep down because of the arthritis in my spine.

I gave her a softer noodle. She still couldn't keep her bottom down and head up, but now it was because of the water!

Customer: The saltwater is what's throwing me off. It makes me too buoyant; too much salt in the water.

This was a colossal shit storm; I had to get her out of the water. I was on deck and literally took her by the hand and towed her into the shallow end. She got to the steps when we were only fifteen minutes into a sixty-minute class. I explained that it would be best that she sticks to land fitness. She really wanted to continue the class, but I insisted it wasn't safe (for either one of us). I convinced her to get out of the pool, but on the second step, she slipped and fell back down. She made a splash, and at that point, I jumped in the water fully clothed to save her in the three feet of water she was in. With visions of my insurance policy dancing in my head, I asked what happened.

Customer: I'm blind in the right eye with no depth perception in the left eye.

She suffered from EFT.
Every Fucking Thing.

Pool Sistas

Judy and I went to a CALA workshop and met two other instructors that worked together. We asked if they were sisters because they looked so much alike. They said, "Not real sisters. We're pool sisters." It stuck with us. Technically, I was the employer and Judy, the employee, but our relationship was based on friendship, and the way we encouraged and confided in each other made us more like sisters. Judy was my very first pool sista!

Judy got her CALA certification at our pool with our group of noodle riding ladies long before I had any plans to start a business at the pool. Fitness and family are her passions, which make the McNeills a very fit family! When I decided to quit accounting and get certified in aqua fit, Judy was my biggest supporter. Over a glass of wine, we would say, "Can you imagine if this aqua fit thing takes off? Maybe you can quit one of your jobs and work at the pool with me. How awesome would that be?!" Judy was working in administration for two high schools, and she wanted out from behind the desk just as much as I had.

With my certification completed and classes starting to fill at the pool, Judy was teaching one night a week with me. A few months later, it was two nights a week. A year later, we were offering more classes, and Judy was able to quit one of her part-time jobs. We kept adding more classes, and they kept filling up. Judy hooked her wagon to my crazy train, and together we left the station, choo choo! She had quit both her jobs, and she was out from behind the desk and up on deck, front and centre!

When it was just the two of us teaching at the pool, we would scrutinize how we taught. It would keep us up at night. Did we have the right music? Was the workout hard enough? Was the workout gentle enough? Were we really good enough to pull this off? The answer was always yes, but the only way we could believe it was to hear it from each other. It's a sister thing.

Judy and I were teaching all the classes we could handle, and there was still a waiting list of people that wanted a spot. We needed another instructor. Roberta was in our classes. She loved aqua fit, loved the pool, and would socially engage with everyone in her class. I invited Roberta to lunch to pitch the idea of her becoming an instructor. She became my second pool sista.

At CALA, they teach us to be "larger than life" on deck. Well, that was our Roberta; she was larger than life on deck. Her visual cues couldn't be missed, and her verbal cues were always witty so as to keep your attention. She was fit, loud, and proud, but the kindness in her heart was her real strength.

Roberta could kick butt at boot camp, but she had a special connection to our older clients, our arthritic clients, and our diabetic clients. Roberta was great on deck, but after class, when she offered encouragement and compassion, she really shined, and so did our aqua fitters. She would relate to everyone and exclude no one. She had a gift. Eventually, the call of her long-horned cattle, organic farming, gardening, and especially her grandkids called her away from the pool and back to her other passions.

You know how sometimes you meet someone for the first time and you just click? That was Sonya and me. We just clicked. We shared the same vision of fitness; it wasn't just for the fit to get fitter or for the fat to lose weight. It wasn't about looking good in a bathing suit. It was about *feeling good*! Sonya is all about lifting spirits. A good workout isn't just the calorie burn. It's connecting, laughing, and walking out in a better mood than you walked in with—and that's what happens when you spend an hour with my pool sista, Sonya!

Every night after the last class ends and everyone has left the building, I close up the pool. I set the timers and temperature controls, turn on the fans, lift mats, and set up to do the whole thing again the next day. Whenever Sonya works nights, there is always a little surprise waiting for me to find while I lock up. It started with a precariously positioned pool noodle on Hulio (a sexy air mattress I keep in the corner), then it was a frog on the teacher's desk. Next was a little pink mermaid sitting on the window ledge, and then there was the turtle on the diving board. The night I found Baby Yoda wrapped in a towel wearing swim goggles nestled on the dumbbell shelf, I knew we had to keep her or him or it—I don't know, I've never watched *Star Wars*. This green-skinned, wide-eyed, big-eared character just seemed to fit right in at the pool. Sonya would move him all over the pool, and I would take pictures of him with our customers. Baby Yoda started as "our thing," but now everyone who comes to the pool is looking for "our thing."

I met Julie when we were both teenagers. We both had boyfriends that were older than us. We thought we were the cool chicks to have older guys (granted, mine didn't have a licence or a car most of the time, but he had an age of majority card!). These days, we wonder how we two hot young chicks got saddled with these two old guys! Just joking; we love old guys (that doesn't sound quite right either, but you know what I mean.)

Julie was teaching spin classes at the YMCA two nights a week, working full time at the high school as an EA for the special needs program, and part-time as a support worker for Community Living. Her schedule left exactly four hours unencumbered. Teaching aqua fit one night a week would button up that time gap perfectly, and another pool sista was found. Julie brought an honest sense of humour to our pool family. From the stories of her family car rides to Puking Lucan (Julie's family suffers car sickness) to her constant "You need to sort that!" She keeps all the sistas laughing.

One day, I walked into my bank and at the wicket was my friend and kindred spirit, Carrie (yes, kindred spirit—I'm also an *Anne of Green Gables* fan!). Carrie had her bank job, but her passion was in fitness. She had become a personal trainer and wanted a career in squats and chin-ups. Carrie had come with me to the annual Fitness Jam, and I knew if the time was ever right, she'd make a great sista! That day in the bank was not a good one for Carrie. There just aren't enough paydays at a job you're not happy at, and that day wasn't payday.

I invited Carrie to lunch. She had never considered aqua fit and wasn't much of a mermaid. I told her to give it some thought and let me know. The next day she sent me an email that she had given her resignation at the bank—this sista thinks fast!

Every instructor, no matter how seasoned and experienced, gets a little nervous before teaching. By the time you're done warm-up, the jitters are gone, unless you're Carrie. She is a fabulous instructor that has the confidence of a beauty contestant entering a Sumo wrestling ring. She knows all the muscle groups, the difference between anaerobic and aerobic exercise, and she walks the walk and can talk the talk, but she was stuck in her head. She needed a sister like me to pull her by the hair, sometimes kicking and screaming, to centre stage where she shines.

Together, all of us pool sisters raised our pool daughter, Mermaid Malyn. Malyn was fourteen years old when I started the aqua fit business. My pool sisters watched her graduate from high school, then college. They met her first boyfriend, her second boyfriend, her third boyfriend… OK, you get where I'm going with this. They were part of her life, and she was part of theirs. Each one had made an impression on her, and I was hopeful that I had too.

After college, Malyn had a diploma in recreational therapy, and she landed a great job at a nursing home in the activities department. She loved her job and the people she worked with, but the smell of chlorine and the sound of splashes were calling her home. She was a training partner for the Red Cross and got her CALA certification in Healing Waters. She could easily make a living at the pool with me, but she needed to march to the beat of her own drum. DrumFIT was her first land fitness certification, then barre, then personal training, then bounce fit. Malyn turned into a new person in just over a year. My pool sisters and I couldn't be prouder!

Together we have the time of our lives on deck and off: goat yoga, axe throwing, kayaking, biking, or just sharing a glance that says, "Don't sweat it, sista; I got you!"

Excuse Me, Can You Pass Me That Nipple?

Sometimes life hands you lemons, and sometimes life hands you breast cancer (makes lemons taste sweet, huh?!) Most of my aqua fitters are women, so breast cancer is a language we speak. My mom had breast cancer, so, I will start with the sad tears, but I promise, happy tears are coming. (If there is a lump in your throat already, don't take a pass on this—tears are just emotions bubbling over. Let them out, or they turn into a tsunami, and no one needs that shit!)

I was a teenager when my mom was diagnosed with breast cancer. She needed her breast removed. Mother of four strong-minded young ladies; she wasn't going into surgery alone (poor Dad with all that estrogen fuming). She had surgery, and all her girls were there in her room after she got out of recovery. Anyone that has been under anesthesia knows how emotional you get out of that tunnel. I only knew my mom to cry when laughing. This was different. No one knew what to do with "this Mom," and that included my dad. He left her room in a hurry with his head in his hands. We girls took the front lines. Dad didn't go AWAL; he went to the florist. He was back with the biggest bunch of yellow roses I'd ever seen. He cried like a baby while he hugged my mom. I was so proud of him.

Mom was released from hospital with home care from VON. She had a nurse come to the house to change her dressing and check the wounds daily. Her nurse was a man named Murray. I have a brother named Murray. What are the chances? Who cares; never look a gift horse in the mouth! Every night at dinner, when my fair-haired, easy-to-blush brother was at the dinner table, someone would ask, "What did Murray think of your breasts today, Mom?" My mom, never to miss an opening, would say, "Murray really liked what he saw!" Laughs all the way round, even from poor Murray.

Are you back on track with smiles? Good, I'm glad.

Years later, I was teaching aqua fit and had participants that had recovered from mastectomies. I always encouraged them not to wear prosthetics in the pool. These women would be so consumed with keeping their boobs in place— not too high, not too low—they weren't listening to me! What the hell? Miss a great workout for the sake of your boobs? Not on my watch.

It was the last class of the evening that I was teaching, and we were doing our stretches, and at the surface of the water, I noticed a single floating nipple happily bobbing away on its own. Unsure if its owner was still in the water, I quietly asked the nearest lady, "Excuse me, could you just pass me that nipple over your right shoulder?"

There I held a lovely C cup breast that went rogue. I made posters for the lost breast (seriously, I made Missing Boob posters). No one claimed her. I introduced her to all the instructors, but no one recognized her (honestly, they all look the same after a few years at the pool). No one ever claimed Betty (yes, we gave her a name: Betty Boob). Betty Boob stayed on the teacher's table in our special little box for a long time. Eventually, like all good boobs, she wrinkled up, lost her bounce, and sagged lower and lower in the box until we all forgot how much fun she was when we first found her.

Life Bridge

I am so glad you made it to this bridge! This is the best bridge to get across. This is what the whole darn trip was about.

You are about to meet some spectacular people who have stories to share that will not only inspire you but encourage you to do a little soul searching of your own. There will be tears on this part of the trip, some from laughter, some not. I am honoured to have met these people, heard their stories, and received permission to share them with you.

Go ahead, turn the pages to go through 2010 to 2021. Take it slow and enjoy the scenery. There are some magnificent views.

I'd Like You to Meet Bert

When I started aqua fit, I took almost every course that CALA had to offer. These courses and conferences got me excited about the healing properties of water, and I was caught hook, line, and sinker (no pun intended). There is scientific evidence that while hydrotherapy will not cure any disease, it is an effective treatment for almost every disease. It is a preferred exercise for anyone with MS that struggles with heat, balance, and flexibility. Water exercise increases range of motion, and that creates synovial fluid to ease arthritis. For heart patients, hydrostatic pressure allows the heart to work more efficiently than it can on land. Buoyancy allows patients with joint replacements to exercise while not bearing weight. I could go on and on (and probably will in later chapters) but suffice to say, water does the body good.

Cindy started coming to my guinea pig classes. She had MS, and her husband Bert suffered from Lyme disease. I was armed and dangerous with all my CALA courses, and confidant water could help them both. We arranged for them to come for a private swim on Friday mornings when I didn't have any other classes booked.

Bert had been misdiagnosed for years, which is common with Lyme, and by the time we met, the disease had taken root in his body. He had trouble walking. All his muscles had tightened and severely restricted his movement in both upper and lower body. His mind was cluttered with a cocktail of medications, his memory was scrambled, and his mood was bleak. A nurse had to come to remove his pick line every time he came to the pool and then put it back in again after. His pain was intense, impossible to predict, and travelled all over his body.

I believe some people have diseases, and some diseases have people; the difference is hope. If you have hope to live your life despite the disease, you have a disease. If you've lost all hope, the disease has you. I didn't know if Bert had Lyme or if Lyme disease had Bert. What I did know was that Bert had Cindy and Cindy had hope.

Bert and Cindy used the pool every Friday morning for an hour. Most days, Bert wouldn't even talk to me. He couldn't, or he wouldn't. The bad days were horrific, and the good days were still awful. His pain, both physical and mental, had a pulse of its own. Cindy never lost patience. My admiration for her grew every week. I was in over my head (pun totally intended) and at a complete loss of how to help Bert. I started dreading Fridays. It was heartbreaking. There was no way I could have known then that Bert and Cindy were going to teach me about water therapy, sickness, love, loyalty and hope, but that's exactly what happened.

A Kiss on the Head

Bert and Cindy continued to come every Friday morning for the first year. Bert would shuffle in wearing his big housecoat, grumbling about how he didn't want to be here, and Cindy would run circles around him to get ready for the pool. By this time, Bert would talk to me a bit, mostly about how much he didn't want to come and how Cindy was making him. He was bitter that Cindy was dragging him to the pool each week, but whenever Cindy was out of earshot, Bert would only sing her praises. If it was just Bert and me, he would talk about how good Cindy was to him, how much he loved her, and how he wouldn't have been alive today if not for her. As soon as Cindy was back within hearing range, he was back to grumbling about being "dragged out to the pool for another near-drowning." I need to be honest here; Bert is a sinker, and by sinker, I mean he is like cement in the water—he goes straight down. There were a few anxious moments when we started therapy swims with Bert, and we were still figuring out which belt or noodle would work best for him, and the only way to find out was to pop him in the water and see if he would sink or float. Cindy and I counted bubbles until eventually, Bert popped back up, gasping for air. We would have saved him. Of course we would have pulled him up eventually, but some days, Bert needed to do things on his own. It was therapeutic (perhaps only for Cindy and me, but therapeutic all the same!).

Lyme disease is an unpredictable condition that can debilitate from head to toe and then disappear for a few weeks, months, or years, only to come back with a vengeance. It affects everyone a little differently physically and psychologically. One Friday morning, Bert was especially harsh with Cindy. It was a bad day for Bert, which made it an even worse day for Cindy. He made some gruff comments to her, and she slipped into the bathroom. While she was out of earshot, Bert told me about a trip they took south, years ago. He never wanted to travel, and she did. She told him, "Either come with me, or I will go alone." He went with her. It was the time of his life. He loved every minute of it and never would have done it without Cindy. He talked about how much he loved her, couldn't imagine a life without her, how strong and smart and self-sufficient she is. I was getting whiplash with Bert's mood swings. In as much time as it took Cindy to go to the bathroom, he went from resentful and angry to grateful and in love. It was dizzying.

There is no way that Cindy could have heard what we were talking about, but when she came out of the bathroom, she walked over to Bert, and she put both her hands on either side of his head. She let her hands slowly slide down the sides of his face to this chin while she gently kissed the top of his head. That kiss forgave everything; it started the day fresh and said all that needed to be said but for which there were no words. It brought me to tears then, and the memory still does now.

Should We Take Bert to the Vet?

We have a loveable, adorable, and incredibly handsome full-size labradoodle. When anyone new meets him, they remark on how handsome he is. He is the kind of dog you expect to see in movies, but he doesn't have time for that; he works full time in the body shop. His name is Wally (short for Walnut), and his coat is a gorgeous walnut brown. He has kind, soulful eyes that make you wonder about all the secrets he carries. If you haven't already guessed, we are a dog family, and Wally is our prince.

Reincarnation is the belief that after you die, you will return to the world in another form. Your rebirth could be in the form of an animal, a human, a plant, or even a spirit. What you return as is a reflection of the life you lived. For example, if you were to return as an animal and you were selfish, cruel, or hurtful, you might come back as a cockroach, something that has a short life and everyone wants to get rid of. If you were kind, generous, and good to people, you might come back as a family pet, something that is cared for and loved. Reincarnation is the Karma of the afterlife. It is a joke in our family that the best possible thing you can be reincarnated to is the Fischtner family dog. Our dogs are showered with love, shampooed with affection, and blown dry with treats, toys, long walks and swims in the pond. So spoiled is our big guy Wally that when he scratches at the door to come in, we open it, and he sits there until we ask, "Do you want a treat?" At which time he walks in and waits for the promised treat; yes, he has trained us well.

Just before Wally's second birthday, he lost his mojo. It started with just a limp for a couple of days, which wasn't surprising from the effort he put into rabbit and mouse hunting. A day later, he was spending most of his time hiding in my closet. That wasn't like him at all. The following day he wasn't using one of his hind legs, and by that afternoon, he wasn't walking. We were carrying our 100-pound prince outside and lifting his leg for him to do his business. We got a vet appointment for that evening; they took blood, ran tests, and sent us home to wait for the results. Wally came home with us.

A couple of hours later, we got a call that Wally had Lyme disease. We were heartbroken. Our only experience with Lyme disease was Bert, and no one wanted Wally to suffer like Bert was suffering. I know that reads badly to compare our dog's situation to Bert's situation, but that is what honesty reads like. We were so upset and imagined a life for our poor Wally riddled with pain and mood swings that would have him hiding in our closets. The vet gave us medication and had us pick it up that evening to start ASAP, they were powerful drugs that we would need to ween him off of over time, but they should help quickly. We weren't as hopeful as our vet. If such drugs did exist, why was Bert still suffering after all these years? That question led to the next one: how is it Wally was diagnosed in less than two hours while Bert waited years for an accurate diagnosis?

The next day was therapy swim with Bert. He knew earlier that week I was worried about Wally. Bert also adored Wally (everyone did). Of course he asked how he was doing. With a lump in my throat and tears filling my eyes, I told him that Wally had Lyme disease. Bert said sorry, and the pained look on his face told me just how sorry he was. Tears filled Cindy's eyes, and we didn't talk about Wally for the rest of that class.

The vet was absolutely right. Within two days, Wally was walking again. A few more days, he was eating, drinking, and back to work as the body shop greeter. Wally goes to work with Ron every morning. He sleeps under his desk, follows him out on the shop floor, and at the sound of the phone ringing, he is the first one back to the office to answer it. Wally made a complete recovery in less than seven days. It was amazing. The medication was expensive but only temporary, and Wally pulled through like a champ. At dinner, we talked about how amazing his recovery was when Malyn had a brilliant idea: how about we give Bert some of Wally's meds? Ronny was quick to point out that Wally needed them to make a full recovery, so Bert should make an appointment with our vet to get some of his own. The kids were young, and that seems laughable, except it's really not.

There is a disconnect in Canada with Lyme disease. I've had four people come to therapy swims with the disease, and while each case is different, their stories are painfully similar. Everyone had gone years with incorrect diagnoses before they were confirmed with Lyme. Everyone had gone years with varying treatment plans and struggled to find a doctor to acknowledge and treat it as Lyme disease. Not only are these people physically suffering, but emotionally they are taking a beating. I had one lady that had to see a therapist once a month so her benefits would cover the cost of her Lyme treatment. Her therapist does not "believe" in Lyme disease. He insists it is all in her head. This woman was in a wheelchair for a year, and her family had to teach her to walk again. That is not in her head! Can you imagine being that sick and in order to get treatment, spend an hour once a month with an educated, registered therapist that has simply decided not to believe in the medically proven disease that you have?

Lyme disease is caused by tick bites. Dogs often attract ticks. They stick to the underside of their belly from running through long grass. Wally has brought home many ticks; we check him nightly and pull them off with special little tweezers we get from the vet. If you have a dog, treat them for ticks, and check them often for bites.

In Canada, we are blessed with free health care. I can't imagine living in a country that you are only as healthy as you can afford to be; that's a terrible thought. At the same time, have we become complacent with our health? When did it become OK to go years misdiagnosed for a disease that can be identified and treated in less than two hours for our four-legged loved ones? Something is missing here. I don't have the answers, but if we don't ask the questions, we never will.

Therapy Swims

Over time, Bert improved. Instead of the occasional good day, he had some good weeks and even months. The pain and the symptoms came back, but they lost some of their strength over him, and he had hope for more good days than bad. He had a disease; it didn't have him anymore. I would love to say it was all thanks to the hour in the pool each week, but it was thanks to medication, his family's support, and perhaps a twist of fate. The pool didn't heal his body, but it served as a good distraction during a very bad time.

As much as I loved having Bert all to myself (almost as much as I love a good root canal), I was getting more calls from people like him that needed some pool time but weren't healthy enough for a regular aqua fit class. I introduced our therapy swims. If you have ever seen the movie, *One Flew Over the Cuckoo's Nest*, imagine that in a pool and I'm Jack Nicholson. Lord help us all.

Therapy swims are for body relief, strength, and flexibility. Everyone works on their own set of exercises that were designed for what their bodies need. Everyone in the pool keeps moving and improving. It is one part exercise, one part social, and when Bert's in the class, one part comedy show, with a little dancing and on his really good days, some singing too (not that he should do either!).

Over the years, I have had several people in our therapy swims. Many of them improve and "graduate" to a regular class. Some stay in therapy for years, making improvements and friends. Sadly, we have lost some friends that were in our swims. My heart breaks a little when a therapy swimmer passes away. I'm so grateful to have met them and that our pool helped relieve their pain while our group made them laugh at least once a week. It takes a village to raise a child *and* to nurture our sick, and love our elders.

How Many Gurneys are we Going Need?

July and August at the pool are for kids' lessons only. We start up adult aqua fit again in September. Every September, we have new people start our programs, and that includes our therapy swims.

It was our first day back to adult classes, and we had two new fellows join our Monday therapy swim. One fellow was nervous about group classes and deep water but was a good swimmer. The other fellow could not swim at all but wasn't nervous for classes; he had Alzheimer's and couldn't remember that he couldn't swim. And then there was Bert.

We started our class the same as usual. I was in the water with them and going over what exercises to do. It was the first week, so I also had Sherrie there to do registration. The new fellow that could swim was pensive but doing fine. The fellow that couldn't swim was with me in the deep end but by the side where he could stay on the ledge and hold the yoga bar. Everyone was safe and doing well until Bert got dizzy—his eyes were like mini slot machines, but instead of going up and down, they went round and round. He wasn't well. We had to get him out of the water, but he was so dizzy that he needed both Cindy and I to guide him out.

My non-swimming Alzheimer client was safely at the side of the pool, on the ledge, holding the bar. My nervous, able swimmer was wide-eyed and looking a little more nervous than when he arrived, but we were in control.

On deck, Bert was getting worse. His heartbeat was racing, and he was too dizzy to stand. He needed an ambulance. This was early days for me, and I hadn't yet learned that when it's time to call an ambulance, it is *not* time to ask your clients permission to call or to negotiate just five more minutes before you call. No one ever wants to call an ambulance or admit they need one. It took about ten minutes to get Bert's permission to call. No harm, no foul in this situation, but waiting is a mistake that I don't make anymore.

The ambulance arrived. The attendants were taking care of Bert and getting him on the gurney. Cindy was gathering their things to leave, and I was explaining to the paramedics what had led up to our situation. Everyone in the swim stayed in the pool; this is the protocol for us. It is much easier for ambulance attendants to work on deck when people aren't on it (yes, this was not our first or last ambulance call). I was visually checking my swimmers, and while they were definitely a little freaked out, there were still four heads above water. They were buckling Bert in and getting ready to head out when my Alzheimer's client decided he wanted to go to the other side of the pool, and to get there, he went right through the middle of the deep end. To his credit, he did make it halfway and then took a dip straight down.

Sherrie: Teresa, should he be doing that?

No, no, no, he should not. In fact, no one should go straight down in the deep end of the pool—I strongly advise against that.

I ran into the pool from the shallow end, and Sherrie jumped in fully clothed from the deep end. We got to him at the same time and together pulled him up coughing, sputtering, and confused that he couldn't swim!

The ambulance attendants were still on deck for this whole shit show.

Me: We're all good. Just take Bert for today!

They made a joke about only having one gurney with them but that they would give a heads up at the station, so everyone knows the quickest route to Over The Deep End. Proud moment, indeed.

Bert suffered from vertigo. He recovered in a couple of weeks. My Alzheimer's client continued to come to classes for a few months, but eventually, he went into a retirement home and had to quit. He was funny and smart, and I'm glad our paths crossed. My nervous swimmer also continued to come to classes. He decided if the first day was that exciting, things could only get better! Sadly, he passed away a few months later from a heart attack. He was quiet, thoughtful, and a pleasure to swim with. As for Bert, the saga continues; seven years later, he still swims weekly. He is the life of the party in the pool. Still a little crusty on the bad days but gives the best hugs on the good days.

Marathons

When I was eleven years old, Terry Fox ran past my house during his Marathon of Hope. I was standing on our front lawn watching the lights and traffic surrounding him when he looked right at me, nodded, and said, "Hi there." I will never forget that day. He was running across the country on one leg, and yes, he was front and centre in my mind that first fateful day of high school when I thought a one-mile run would kill me. I was in complete awe of him; until I met Pam Peeters.

Pam was born with cystic fibrosis, a disease that causes the airways and lungs to fill with mucus and make breathing difficult. There is no cure. Pam needed a double lung transplant. Her life was in the hands of one of the less than twenty percent of Canadians that sign their organ donor cards. A single donor can help as many as seventy-five people and save up to eight lives, and yet only twenty percent of us plan to be organ donors. She got the call. She was at the top of the list, and they had a match. I have to stop and pause here. Imagine right now as you inhale and exhale, just imagine that simple action that we do all day long without so much as a second thought. Imagine it being so difficult that the only alternative is to have your lungs taken out of you and someone else's put in. It baffles me that breathing could be so difficult and that medical science is so amazing.

Her surgery was a success, her body accepted the lungs, and she could breathe. Doctors were unsure if she had an allergic reaction to the anti-rejection drugs or if cystic fibrosis had attacked her spinal cord after her lungs were removed; either way, the result was that at forty years of age, Pam could breathe, but now she couldn't walk.

I met Pam at the pool. She had been using a therapy pool in London while she was still in recovery, but now she had to find her own water therapy. We don't have a chair lift or a ramp for our pool, but that wasn't going to stop Pam. We don't have wheelchair parking or automatic doors, but that wasn't going to stop Pam. I had never worked with anyone confined to a wheelchair, and that didn't even make her flinch.

Pam was able to get herself into a standing position, and then I would work her feet to get down the steps. I'm not going to lie, it wasn't pretty in the beginning, but now, years later, we move together like professional dancers (dancers with two left feet wearing clown shoes). The first time she got in the water, she was able to walk the length of the pool holding a noodle at the surface. Her moves were jerky and took all the energy she had, and it was freaking amazing! It was another Terry Fox moment for me—I was in awe of her.

We got her in the deep end and tethered her to the wall. If she could walk, then she could run, and run she did. She was coming to the pool three times a week and getting stronger all the time. Of course, she joined Bert's therapy class; she had two therapy swims a week and one regular aqua fit class. I love it when she arrives at a new class in her chair, and everyone in the water wonders, "How the hell are they going pull this off?" and then we do. She quietly has the respect of everyone in the water, no matter what class she is in. It is no big deal, just Pam taking an aqua fit class. She inspires a lot of people.

Every year at the pool, we host a "Water Running Marathon." It is a fundraiser, and each year, we pick a new charity. It is a one-day event that people sign up for a forty-five-minute time slot in the pool for which they water run the entire time. We have instructors on deck to help motivate and good tunes to keep them on pace to water run five kilometres in the forty-five minutes. It is a pool party with a purpose. We raise money and awareness for charities that tend to go unnoticed. It is always a pretty magical day. When Pam started coming to our classes, I asked if she wanted a spot in our marathon, and of course she did. Not only did Pam want a spot, but she also put together a team of water runners and got pledges for our charity. I was always proud of our water running marathons but never prouder than when Pam rolled through the doors.

Life can feel like it's really slapping me around sometimes, and I have two good legs. Every time I think of Terry Fox or dance Pam into the pool, I'm not just thankful for my good health, but I'm thankful for theirs. People with different abilities are people with different opportunities for greatness.

Nipples, Nipples, Everywhere

With 300 women a week in and out of bathing suits, you're going to see some nipples. Some shrivelled hanging low, some with the high beams on, some that make you jealous, and some that make you feel blessed. As an aqua fit instructor, if you've seen one, you've seen them all. It's no biggie. Well, actually, that's not true—there are *really* big ones too!

An incredible advantage that water training has over land training is called the Blanket Effect. The Blanket Effect is only achieved in deep water. When you submerge in deep water, the only part of your body visible is from the neck up. It's a pretty awesome way to see each other. No bling, no eying each other up and down, no judgement. It is like being under a blanket that is tucked up under your chin; you feel safe and covered. You see everyone in your class the same way that they see you, head and shoulders only, unless you're the instructor. We see it all, the jiggle, the wiggle, and who needs to shave.

Wardrobe malfunctions happen, and when it happens in a pool of warm water, it can go undetected for a painfully long time. I was teaching a boot camp class and had two teams in the water doing races. It was a competition, and the first team to get all its players back in the shallow end won. When the last member of the winning team crossed the finish line, she jumped up and raised both arms in the air with a triumphal "Woo Hoo!" One breast decided to make an escape at that moment. She high-fived all her teammates with a one-eyed monkey on her chest. No one noticed or cared—they'd won the race!

If I notice a boob peeking out from behind the curtain, I make every attempt to discreetly notify the stage crew. Sometimes the stage crew doesn't listen to the director, and the boob steals the show altogether.

We often do circuits in the pool; there are stations set up all along the parameter of the pool, each with a different exercise to be done. Everyone is at a different spot, and they do one minute of each exercise and then move to the next station. There is always chatter during circuit classes; there is no instructor to talk over, so it's a good time for small talk in the pool. I noticed everyone was avoiding one lady. They weren't talking to her, and some were even turning their backs to her to avoid eye contact. She was at the back wall of the pool, so I couldn't see her face to see if she had noticed the cold shoulder her classmates were giving her. As soon as she turned the corner to face me, I saw the problem: one nipple took jump squats up a notch and jumped out of her suit! Ugh, this was going to be awkward, and I had to get to her before she got to the steps. The step circuit is in the shallow end, and you have to go up and down the first step as quickly as possible. You are only in waist-high water and bouncing. Both her girls needed to be strapped back in before that station. I made eye contact with her and gestured her bathing suit strap.

She smiled and waved back.

I crouched down and, as quietly as possible, said, "Your bathing suit needs adjusting."

She smiled and laughed back; she couldn't hear me over the music. I tried charades. I physically tucked my own boob into my sports bra. At this, she really laughed, and to be honest, I do some weird shit on deck, and that move wasn't entirely out of character for me. It was time for her to go to the step; there was no way she wouldn't notice the inequality of her bounce at that station. Damn! That nipple bounced through a full minute on the step. It was mocking both of us, and at this point, everyone in the pool was pulling up their own straps and looking at me with an expression of "Do something about this, *now*!"

I stopped her after the step and said, "Hey, your boob is out."

She looked down and was the only one in the room to be surprised by what she saw. I talked to her after class and sympathetically said, "Hey, shit happens—it's just a boob." I don't think she felt the same. She quit classes shortly after that.

The pool is kept at eighty-eight degrees, and the room is always hot and humid. Getting dressed out of a wet bathing suit in a hot, humid change room can burn as many calories as the aqua fit class. We run through the winter, so dashing home in a towel isn't always an option. However, wearing a bra is completely optional! Bras are the hardest part of getting dressed, and everyone starts classes with dignity and proper attire, but as they exhaust themselves and get more comfortable, the bra is the first to go. I know a new customer will become a long-term customer when she comes jiggling out of the change room saying, "To hell with my bra, I'm going home like this!"

In the words of the great late Helen Reddy, "I am woman hear me roar."

Speedo Class

What kind of man takes aqua fit classes? A confident one!
I have precious few men in our classes, and even though
I take a special kind of pleasure in beating the life out of
them in the water, I have the utmost respect for these
strong, confident men. Aqua fit is typically thought of as
"your grandma's exercise class," and that's just not true! Men
are the same as women, and their joints snap, crackle, and
pop the same as women. Aqua fit is a non-weight bearing
exercise that means no pressure on the joints. We are not a
bunch of old ladies doing egg beaters sitting at the edge of
the pool. We are water-running, Tabata-training, and cardio-
boxing men and women kicking ass in a liquid gym. Don't
believe me? Come to my class.

Our first male aqua fitter was Wayne Moore. When
Wayne called to inquire about classes, I was quick to explain
that I currently had no men in any of our classes. He said,
no problem—he didn't mind women in the pool. I thought
either he was a pervert looking to score at the pool, or
he was a guy ahead of his time, ahead of his gender, and
someone I want to meet. Good news: Wayne's not a perv!
I could put Wayne in any class. He would fit in with boot
camp babes, he would welcome new people to beginner's

classes, and go with the flow in any gentle class. He naturally put people at ease, and eventually, his wife joined him in classes too.

One of my boot campers, Michelle, wanted to buy her partner Ken a gift certificate for aqua fit classes as a Valentine's Day gift. *Fabulous* gift. What says "I love you" more than an exercise class that will keep you healthy, happy, and flexible (wink, wink, nudge, nudge). I suggested he try one class before she bought him a full session. Thursday 11:00 a.m. with Wayne; if that didn't hook him, nothing would. Ken was nervous about his first class. He knew Ron, so he came early that Thursday and went to the auto body shop first for a little intel on aqua fit classes. Ron was absolutely no help at all. Ken asked what he should expect. Ron was honest: he had never been to one of my classes. True, he walked past the window several times a day and saw me "dancing" on deck, but he had no idea what I did. All he could tell Ken was that those women drag their asses to their cars exhausted after class, and every week, they come back smiling and excited to be here again. Crazy shit.

It didn't make Ken feel any better to find out Ron had never been to my class; I had a waiting list, and he hadn't even taken one class? Ron sensed that Ken was going to bolt, and if he did, I would most certainly blame Ron for it; this would not fare well for my husband. Ron promised Ken if he liked the class and decided to join, then Ron would too. I am certain that Ron never thought for a minute that Ken would like the class and sign up for a permanent spot the following week.

Ken joined the class, and a few weeks later, Ron did too! We call them the Speedo Class, and all the instructors are very thankful they don't wear Speedos. They work hard, laugh loud and can all agree I am their least-liked instructor. Some of the characters have changed over the years, but Wayne, now with two knee replacements and a heart bypass, is still the Captain of the Speedo Class!

Sister Wives

Don't judge me. I have to be honest: I love my sister wives.

Polygamy is one husband and more than one wife. I think that's just ridiculous. My poor husband would crumble like a cookie trying to keep more than one woman happy, and I'm not the kind of woman to share my man! However, wouldn't it be great to have help raising your kids, prepping your meals, shopping with you, and rooting for you all the time? Husbands try, and try hard, but women have an innate knowledge of caring for others. There is a lot of caring to be done on a daily basis, and this is where my sister wives come in!

I'll start with my beauty and shopping sister wife, Deb. I hate shopping. I know most women love shopping and, trust me, I am a woman, but shopping *sucks*. I've avoided shopping most of my adult life. For my college graduation, I borrowed a friend's bridesmaid's dress. For my wedding, I bought the first dress I tried on. For Malyn's graduation, we planned a dress shopping trip. It started with "just try it," and a few stores later it became, "Put It *On!*"

That was followed by an uncomfortable situation when a sales lady asked, "Can I help you?"

To which I replied, "Do you have a black dress that isn't dark? It can't have sleeves and not be sleeveless. It must be above the knees but not slutty. Floral is an absolute *no,* but solids are out too. No time for alterations, so we need a perfect fit. Go ahead, pull that off your freaking shelf."

The day ended with, "If you don't pick a dress, I am not taking you home. We will sleep in the car if we have to." She picked a dress. It's still in my closet, never worn.

Malyn's high school prom was coming up, and she needed a formal dress, and I needed a sister wife. Deb is all things girly, so I invited Deb for a day of dress shopping. The first shop we went to and the first dress Malyn tried on was perfect. It fit, it was beautiful, it was available, and I thought we were done. Malyn insisted she keep trying on more dresses. I thought that was ridiculous—we found a dress; let's go home. This is where having a sister wife was crucial. Deb agreed with Malyn: she can't possibly buy the first dress she tried on. Now we have a dress to compare all the others to. No arguments, no name-calling, and no scenes with the lovely dress shop ladies, all thanks to my sister wife, Deb. We went to numerous shops that day, and Malyn tried on countless dresses, and then we went back to the first shop and bought the first dress. What seemed like a complete waste of a day to me was time well spent, according to Deb. Malyn didn't just need a dress. She needed to feel like a princess, and that, my dear, takes time.

Next up is my soup sister wife, Barb. We love soup. Ron eats it twice a day most days. That's a lot of soup. Ronny and I can make a meal out of a bowl of soup, but for Ron it's still an appetizer. I do all the cooking in our house (Ron sticks to breakfast while sipping his cup of hot bacon fat). That makes for a lot of soup-making. Who has time for all that soup? My sister wife, Barb, does. Besides my mom, she makes the best soup. I just let her know what kind and how much soup we need, and she brews it up for us. In return, I'm her aqua fit sister wife. She makes my husband happy twice a day, and in return, twice a week, I keep her healthy and limber, which keeps her husband happy (although I doubt it's twice a day!).

My third sister wife is Lori. She's my cheerleader. Lori is the wife that always boosts my spirits and pumps me up when I feel deflated. When I wanted to do a 5km run, she said, "Let's do it." When I wanted to do a triathlon, she said, "Sure. I'll give it a try." When I did a duathlon without her, she drove two hours to surprise me on route, holding up a sign to cheer me on. Lori has never said no to anything I've asked: concerts, road trips, fitness challenges, sewing mermaid costumes, and even educating Malyn and her friend Lindsey on the finer arts and culture of male strippers. She's the *yes* wife. If you only have one sister wife in your life, find a *yes* wife!

My last sister wife is my silent sister wife, Barb. Yes, I know what you're thinking: *Four wives and two of them are named Barb? Wouldn't that get confusing?* Not really. Barb and Barb are really good friends and are often together, so it's actually easier for me—I just say Barb, and they both think I'm talking to them, much less jealousy about who's my favourite Barb this way. Barb is quiet and sincere. She says the kindest things and makes small gestures that mean big things. Barb is also the dog-walking wife. She has never had a dog but thinks walking them would be fun. I have two labradoodles that have a combined weight of 150 pounds. That's a lot of fun on a leash!

I met all these ladies at the pool. They started as customers, became friends, and now they're my sister wives. They make me feel safe and supported, and they do it effortlessly. You know what they say, "Happy wife, happy life." It's true, ladies. Go out and get yourself a wife!

Survive, Celebrate, and Swim!

Every year, we take the month of December off from adult aqua fit classes at the pool. I use this time to recharge my batteries, and I sometimes need to put my booster cables on someone else's battery.

There was a year at the pool that we had a lot of customers battling cancer. One of my sister wives was diagnosed with breast cancer. She shared with me what a cancer diagnosis really felt like, the decisions that she had to make, and the emotions she had to navigate her family through. She said there should be a cancer mentorship program; there is so much treatment information available, but what she needed was human shoulders to lean on and some honest, "been there, done that" accounts to help her make decisions.

In December, I hosted a Survive, Celebrate, and Swim and invited cancer survivors, cancer patients, and their caregivers for a swim and a sense of community. Yes, a real Mother Teresa here, right? Wrong. Those ladies were the saints, and I was the one with a dead battery. I heard stories of survival that brought me to tears, and I felt a friendship and sisterhood that charged my battery full.

There was a woman that had fought both breast and lung cancer. There were survivors of cervical cancer, bone cancer, and one woman that had just been diagnosed with non-Hodgkin's lymphoma. Some were still in the fight, and some were cheerleading from the finish line; all of them shared a strong spirit, and together they could share in a way that no one else could. My mother fought cancer three times: bone, breast, and thyroid. I missed her that day. She would have been my guest of honour.

One of my aqua fitters shared with me what it was like to tell her daughter she had breast cancer. She said, "Remember when you were a kid, and you did something really bad, and you knew it was bad, and you *had* to tell your parents? You knew how disappointed they would be, and there was no way around it." If you can read that without getting a knot in your belly, you, my friend, have forgotten a portion of your childhood (put the wine glass down—now!). I could feel exactly what she was talking about: that terrible feeling of knowing you were going to disappoint or hurt someone that loved you. Not only did she have to deal with her own emotions of a cancer diagnosis, she had to mother up and help her daughter deal with it. Not fair.

I offered the pool to her and her family for a private little buoyancy moment away from cancer and hospitals. Years later, I was on the phone with someone from my bank, and through small talk, I figured out *she* was the daughter. She and I had never met, but she remembered her time in the pool, and I remembered her mom sharing her diagnosis with me. Both she and her mom were doing great, and little did either of them know, they charged my battery then and again years later in some friendly small talk. Small talk isn't small unless you're not really listening.

The Sweet Diabetes Class

What can aqua fit do for diabetics? Damn near everything! Physical exercise works sugar out of muscles. The lowered blood sugar level can last for up to twenty-four hours if that exercise is vigorous enough in both cardio and muscle endurance. Hydrostatic pressure pushes all the fluids in the lower extremities upward. Diabetics often suffer from swollen feet and ankles that stop them from getting enough exercise. In the water, they don't have to bear weight, and it reduces the swelling for up to twenty-four hours. That's the physical benefits, but the real payoff is a friendship sweeter than a homemade butter tart.

I have to give a big shout-out to the Strathroy Diabetes Education Centre. Those ladies know how to advocate for their clients. When my classes started, the nurse from the Diabetes centre called to request I do a class specifically for their patients. At the time, I was in over my head: too many classes, too many people on a waiting list, and I was swimming in administration instead of my pool. I explained that I couldn't help right now. Six months later, they called again, and I was still too busy to help. A year later, they called again. I explained that we were just shutting things down for the summer break. They weren't going away. They offered to do all the registration for a trial class to spare me the administration time. They suggested we do it during our summer break so as to not interrupt the regular class schedule. For every "No, I can't..." that I had, they had a "Yes, we can..." And they were right. Together we could, and we did.

We did one class for them to try. Some of them couldn't swim, some of them struggled to walk, but everyone loved it! We didn't need a diabetes class. We needed two diabetes classes. They loved the warmth of the water and moving with ease. They were hooked, and so was I. There is no doubt aqua fit is fun, but when you can do something fun and improve someone's health, it gives you a natural high, and I'll just say it—I like getting high!

All the instructors work on a rotating schedule. This way, we all get to teach each class at some point in the session. For some reason, I have a reputation for being the "tough" instructor. It's bullshit, really. I'm a sweetheart on deck! Anyways, it was my turn to teach the diabetes classes, and they were nervous; they had heard the rumours. I gave them all a good workout, and by the time we got to stretch, I was playing nice and making friends again.

There is one stretch that we hang on to the yoga bars and drop our hips. On deck, we hold the equipment shelf to demonstrate the pose. To compensate for the ass-kicking I just gave them, I was really turning on the charm for stretch. I demonstrated at the shelf and then walked to the other side of the pool to accommodate the people at that wall.

The only thing I had to hang on to was a window crank. *Well, that should work*, I thought. In my calmest voice and gentle movements, I had one hand on the crank, lifted the other hand overhead and let my body weight fall towards the pool. If you've ever wondered how much weight a window crank can carry, let me tell you, not enough to keep my ass on deck! I went straight into the pool, ass first. I bobbed back up, took a breath, and without missing a beat, finished the stretch. All the ass-kicking was forgotten. I just made eight friends that would be swimming with me for years.

One year we had a contest called Get Your Ass to Class. We took attendance at every class for six weeks, and the classes with the best attendance won T-shirts. Both diabetes classes walked out with T-shirts that year; they loved their aqua fit classes. We had two full classes for our diabetes group. They were dedicated to their classes.

Twice a year, the Diabetes Education Centre would send a nurse out to test blood before and after classes. On average, every participant's blood glucose would drop two to five levels after a forty-five-minute aqua fit class. The higher their blood glucose was before class, the more significant the drop was after class. For all the instructors, it validated what we were doing and how hard we were working.

I was teaching the diabetes class the week before the scheduled glucose tests. I told the classes that the nurse would be here the following week for blood tests. I was excited and figured they would be too. The following week

I went out to see how things were going, and there sat the nurse and my instructor—not a single person came to class. This was the same class that won the attendance contest. What the heck?!

I didn't understand it then, but I do now. They live with diabetes 24-7. Every day is determined by blood tests, insulin, and diet. For one hour a week at the pool, they were just a group of people exercising pain-free and sharing laughs. They didn't want their blood tested; they wanted an hour of living without diabetes, and in the pool, they got it!

We don't need blood tests to validate what we do. The smiles shining up at us are all the validation we need.

A Word on Weight Loss

I know a lot of people that have struggled with weight loss for most of their lives. I know one lady that was always a little chunky as a kid and gained a bit more with childbirth and a bit more at her office job, and no matter how hard she tried, she just couldn't get the scale to reflect her efforts. That was me, and it drove me crazy. Ron used to say the most unattractive thing about me is how I see myself. It pains me to say this, but he was right (not that I lacked self-confidence, but that he was actually *right* about something).

My kids were both picky eaters. Luckily, Ronny grew out of it and kicked the toast and jam addiction once and for all (still not a fan of mild Italian sausage though). Malyn's addiction was pizza: cheese pizza—nothing but cheese, sauce and crust—no toppings. That was her go-to for breakfast, lunch, and dinner if she could swing it. My rule was the kids had to try whatever I cooked at least seven times before deciding they either liked or disliked it. For Malyn, trying meant taking one bite-size piece, smelling it, fondling it, turning her nose up at it, dissecting it, and eventually feeding it to the dog or throwing it in the garbage at least seven times.

Malyn was a tough customer at the dinner table. Her aversion to trying new foods and making a steady diet of cheese pizza was putting pounds on that weren't healthy for her at such a young age. If you're a parent, you know that talking to your kids about weight loss can be harder than talking to them about sex. We understand and enjoy sex, but weight loss is still such a mystery and what's there to like about it? It was a constant battle between keeping her healthy or keeping her confident—she deserved both.

After years of trying to diet and ramp up her exercise, all that changed was her waistline and not in the direction we were hoping for. I always believed that to lose weight, you need to forget whatever the latest fad is and just eat less and move more. Malyn was eating less, but it was still cheese pizza, and moving more, but it was joyful movement—not the kind that leaves you sore and breathless. When she was twenty years old, I included her in an online workshop about setting goals and achieving them. She attended it. She made herself a vision board, and on that board was a mini clothesline with mini clothespins. Each pin represented one pound that she wanted to lose. She started asking me for help with her meal planning instead of avoiding running into me in the kitchen. She started exercising several times a day, every day, and day after day, she was taking the clothespins off her vision board.

Malyn went to a completely plant-based diet; kale and spinach were her new best friends. Cauliflower steak and stir fry were her treat meal. Cheese pizza was her past.

She gained a new respect for food and what it can do *for* you instead of *to* you. She had spent twenty years eating her anxiety, so there was some work to be done in that department too.

She started her land fitness classes. Her first certification was as a DrumFIT instructor. Classes were filling and excitement growing, and then COVID shutdown number one. She used that shutdown to work on her own weight loss. Fifty-four pounds later, she was ready to offer classes again. Classes resumed with smaller groups and distancing. She had to teach behind a plexiglass screen and clean all the equipment between each use. Tough way to make a living, but she was happy to return to the living. She had twelve weeks in, and then COVID shutdown number two happened. She used that shutdown to get certified as a barre instructor. Classes resumed again: smaller groups yet, but hey, we were working. Then COVID shutdown number three—time for Malyn to finish her certification as a personal trainer.

It took a worldwide pandemic for this little girl to find herself, and what a find that turned out to be! She loved her body the way she'd always loved her friends and her family. The girl with the voice of an angel had a new song to sing! She had learned so much about food and nutrition (yes, they are two *very* different things) and exercise that it was hard to believe she had lived on cheese pizza for years. She inspired a lot of people, and some reached out to her. "How did you do it? No, really. What did you take to lose all that weight? Tell me. I won't tell anyone else." She didn't "take" anything, she ate her damn vegetables, and you can tell *everyone!*

Eating clean and exercising hard worked for Malyn, but it doesn't work for everyone...

I have a friend that came to our classes who had been overweight since childhood. She tried numerous diets and exercise plans. She was focused, goal-oriented, and determined, but no matter what she did, the weight wouldn't drop. She was considering gastric bypass surgery. I was discouraging her from doing something so severe to her body. My mindset has always been to eat clean and move; your body knows what to do when you send it the right messages. She had a young family and wanted to be a role model for them and feel more comfortable in her own skin. She decided on surgery. I told her, "I support *you.* If this is the right thing for you, then I support that." But in all honesty, I had doubts that she was doing the right thing. She had lived overweight most of her life, and that meant she knew what body shaming felt like and how often and easy it was for everyone else to assume her weight was the result of overeating and laziness. She showed me a five-minute video that explained how our environment has seriously changed our metabolism and made weight loss so much harder. I knew she was active in her work and in raising her young family. I knew how much she ate: it was very little. I would never survive on so little, yet I still believed she needed to eat less and move more. I was wrong. It doesn't work for everyone, and to make matters worse, I was discouraging her from a solution that would end the madness.

She had the surgery and dropped over a hundred pounds. She smiles more, laughs louder, and has given me a whole new perspective on weight loss. I'm not saying surgery is the solution for everyone, but it is the solution for some, and who the hell am I to judge them?

The last person anyone would expect me to write about in this chapter is my pool sista, Judy. Judy has the body you'd expect to see on the cover of a fitness magazine with a flashy title like "Six Pack Abs and Sexy Arms into your Sixties!" Judy is a lean, mean, muscle machine, so why is she in the chapter about weight loss? It's because this chapter isn't really about weight loss, is it? It's about how we see ourselves and others.

Judy came to an aqua fit class that I was teaching. Instructors jump into classes when there is room. Judy liked morning boot camps, and I always like having instructors in my class. She got in the water and made a comment that she really needed a good workout that day, after eating and drinking all weekend. There were several women in the water that rolled their eyes at Judy's comment. One lady even questioned her on it. "*You* need a good workout? Ya right!" Judy was offended, and we talked about it after class. She said it's not fair to assume weight control was any easier for her than it was for anyone else. At the time, I thought bullshit. She was so thin and fit; it had to be easier for her. I've worked out with Judy, and I've shared a lot of meals and wine with Judy. It's not any easier for her. Everything is a choice. We all have to make choices.

When I changed careers from accounting to aqua fit, I dropped some unwanted pounds and welcomed some new muscle. The biggest change came when I realized that judgment is like powdered sugar donuts: zero nutritional value and too much will make you sick.

Fearful, Faithful Helen

Whenever someone new wants to join our aqua tribe, I ask if they are fearful of deep water. I have been through this with enough people now that I can decode their answers. If they say they're not swimmers but like water, chances are they're fine. If they hesitate and say "not really," then they really are a little fearful. If they say, "What do you mean by *deep* water? *How* deep?" their bowels are going loose and just talking to me about deep water is making their heart race.

My friend Helen started classes with us before I learned to decode, and little did I know, she was scared. Helen was retired from a church where she worked as a grief counsellor and pastoral minister. Her soft voice, calm demeanour, and sincerity made her very good at what she did. Her faith gave others strength when they needed it most.

When Helen called to inquire about classes, she told me that she didn't know how to swim. I said, "No problem." Often non-swimmers do better in aqua fit because they stay vertical, whereas swimmers naturally want to move through the water in a more horizontal swimming formation. When she came to her first class, I fitted her for a belt and suggested she take a spot in the back row nearest the shallow end for the first few classes until she got more comfortable. This spot became known as Helen's spot.

Helen entered the pool and was smiling in the shallow end; she had been on the waiting list for a long time before getting into one of our classes—she was savouring this moment. I walked beside her on deck to show her where the slope to the deep end was, and off she went, Over The Deep End! Then right back she came into the shallow end! She was scared of deep water, very scared. She didn't want to give up. After all, if Jesus could walk on water, then certainly she could swim in it!

Again, she ventured into the deep end, this time gripping the wall and with me coaching beside her on deck. I got her to the first bar and tethered her. I told her to hang on to the bar with one hand until she felt confident to let go. She needed to trust her belt to keep her afloat and engage her core to stay vertical. She'd be fine.

I was the instructor for that class, and Helen held that bar for dear life all through the warm-up. Getting into the cardio, I gently said, "If you want to let go of the bar now, Helen, you can."

She gave me a warm smile and a decisive shake of her head, no. From cardio, we moved into muscle work. Everyone had two buoyancy dumbbells, one to hold in each hand. Now Helen would have to let go of the bar to hold her weights. Nope. Helen took one weight in one hand and kept the other hand on the bar. To work both sides, she would move the weight from one hand to the other but never without having a hand on the bar. *OK*, I thought, *she's taking her time finding her water legs. No problem*. The last half of the class is done un-tethered and travelling in the pool. For this, Helen would have to let go of the bar. I was wrong again. Helen decided to stay tethered and hold the bar for the entire class. Everyone else simply travelled around her. It was a great opportunity for her to meet everyone.

Helen stayed stuck on that bar for almost a year. She rarely missed a class, and if someone new was taking a spot in that class, everyone would make it clear which spot was Helen's and that it was off-limits to anyone else. Eventually, Helen let go of the bar but wouldn't stray far from it and wouldn't untether. As her confidence grew, she kept getting braver. Fearful, faithful Helen was a free-wheeling aqua fitter in less than three years (and for the record, that is the longest I've ever seen anyone persevere deep water). She had her spot "reserved at the bar" for two classes a week. I was so impressed that someone at her stage in life would overcome deep water fear. It took my breath away. Sadly, it was Helen's breathing that was a problem.

Since starting classes, Helen became more active and fit—she was what I like to call Senior Strong. Then she had some breathing troubles, extended colds, and was generally feeling unwell. She was still coming to class but now with a cane, not because she couldn't walk; she couldn't breathe. She had to take breaks just walking from the car to the pool to catch her breath. She was getting winded after any kind of exertion. Eventually, she was diagnosed with blood clots in her lungs. Her lungs were not functioning properly. Surgery was required but came with many risks and could only be done in Toronto. Without surgery, Helen would continue to deteriorate. Faithful Helen put her trust in the hands of the surgeons, and with her family by her side and God in her heart, she made her way to Toronto.

Helen suffered a stroke during the surgery. Things had gone from bad to worse, but just like at the pool, Helen hung on for as long as it took to get Senior Strong again. It took two years to recover; she had to learn to walk again and suffered many setbacks along the way. Her family literally supported her every step of the way, and eventually, Helen made it back to the pool.

With her driver's licence revoked because of the stroke, she was dependant on others to get to the pool. Her daughter brought her to the first class; I couldn't believe what I saw. Helen looked fabulous, years younger despite the cane and slower movements. She got in the water, and instead of gripping nervousness, I could see her shoulders relax, her eyes smile, and her spirit soar. Helen had taken a journey few of us are challenged to take, and few of us would have the endurance to walk away from.

Helen now drives herself to class again. She has faithfully gone from fearful to fearless. Praise the Lord!

Kicking Ass at Class

We have over forty adult aqua fit classes a week at the pool. Some of the groups have been together for years, and each class develops a "personality." All the instructors are on a rotating class schedule. Each has their "regular" class that they teach more often than any others, but every instructor teaches each class at some point in the session. Over the years, we have found it easier to give some of our classes little nicknames to help us remember what "personality" of class we are instructing.

Our nickname system started with the Posties. We had a group of women that were either retired or still working at Canada Post. We have all heard the saying, "Don't go postal!" well, these ladies make me want to go postal all day long! These ladies work hard and come to the pool to work even harder. They swear like old sailors, care for each other with all their hearts, and make me laugh until tears run down my legs.

Another class became known as the Barely Breathing. At our staff meeting, we were talking about how hard it was to motivate this group to get moving. One instructor said, "I wonder if we should take their pulse before they get in the water?" After a round of giggles, we termed them the

Barely Breathing. Don't get us wrong; we love this group just like any other. It's humbling for all of us to spend an hour a week looking at our future. I hope that we are all lucky enough to get to their age and still be taking aqua fit. Bravo to the Barely Breathing (and no, of course it's not the class you're in!).

Me and My Pals class was introduced when we first started. Basically, if you had enough friends to put together your own class, you could have a Me and My Pals class. These are my favourite classes to teach; everyone is happy to see each other and catch up on life that they hardly notice I've added an extra five minutes to the cardio side of class. One of our Pals classes gets together for dinner during the Christmas season, and they even invite me. Most of the ladies in this group have been friends since kindergarten, and now I was one of their honorary pals!

Another Pals class had a fun bunch of ladies with different backgrounds who had been coming to class together for six years. They had celebrated weddings, births, and retirements together, and then there was one cancer diagnosis that changed everything. Kim was in that class, and she was the quiet, smiling glue that helped hold the group together. She came to classes as long as she could through treatments, but when she passed away a year later, the group wasn't the same. A couple of ladies moved to an earlier timed class, and a couple switched to a different day. Everyone in that group still comes to classes but not together. A Pal's class needs all its pals. She was missed, and a replacement wasn't going to make that feeling go away.

At the pool, we have a lot of teachers taking classes. Not sure what it is about aqua fit that is so appealing to teachers, but they come to the pool in droves. The instructors all joke that teaching teachers is the worst! They don't listen, they talk during class, they constantly ask you to repeat the instructions, and they are the most likely to forget their towel. I'm not sure if it's a role reversal that happens when that last bell rings at the end of the day, but shit, these ladies make us work for it at class, and we love them!

Then there are the retired teachers; let me introduce Sandi. When I started the aqua fit business, I did classes for free to get people interested. She came to one of those classes. She arrived with her own belt and had already taken a class that morning in London. No one had come to my class with their own belt, and most people had never taken an aqua fit class in their life, never mind earlier the same day. I was going to have to step up my game here a bit. Sandi listened to every word I said on deck. I'm big on proper posture and holding good form in the water, and Sandi *wanted* to have good form in the water. She spent a few hours every week in the water. Now, she was learning how to get the most out of that time.

Sandi became our TA (teacher's aid) in classes. When I have someone new starting or someone fearful of water, they start in Sandi's class. Sandi helped fearful, faithful Helen, and danced Pam into the water a time or two. She has helped with the Sweet Diabetes class and our Special Needs class. She has baked sweets for all our staff parties, knitted socks, hats, and mittens for everyone in my family and is part of that "something" you can't put your finger on that makes Over The Deep End so special.

Thursday night classes are the Aqua Warriors. I don't know what happens to this group all week, but by the end of it, these ladies come to the water running and punching like their lives depend on it. Our regular adult aqua fit season ends in June, and for our last class, we celebrate by enjoying sangrias and nachos with the last class of the evening on Thursday. Over the years, the people in the last class of the night have changed, but every time I serve sangrias and nachos, we sit, talk, laugh, and it's a little magical. It feels like we can solve the world's problems, end inequality and racism, and find and give support to those who need it. All this with only a pitcher of sangrias, a plate of nachos, and a group of like-minded women. (Don't underestimate the power of my sangrias; they have taken many by surprise).

I knew I hit it big time in my fitness career when a rebel sixty-year-old redhead said she was getting a tattoo on her arm that read, "Teresa's Bitch." This was made even more impressive by my belief that she was a lesbian. Wow, I really have it—I don't even have to swing both ways to bat 'em out of the park.

Lunch bag let down, she's not gay, she just "Fucking Loves Me."

Irene and Kathy are a couple of my favourite aqua fitters that swim twice a week in my pool of favourite aqua fitters. Irene started classes with us and then brought her "friend" Kathy. These two ladies drove to class together, lived "next door" to each other, and carried each other's water bottles and towels to class for each other. All of the instructors agreed: they must be lovers. Good for them, stepping out of their comfort zone in a small-minded small town, or so we thought. Shame on us. These two incredible, genuine golden girls were not lesbians (much to their husbands' relief). They were best friends that actually lived next door to each other. They had a friendship stronger than family ties, more precious than gold, and possibly the best example of true friendship for my pool sistas and me. Karma again.

Kathy wears her emotions on her sleeve with an "F" bomb. Irene is organized and would give you the shirt of her back if you needed it. Together they make Over The Deep End better. We always joke that they are my "favourite" aqua fitters. One day Kathy asked if they really could be my favourites. I answered, "Of all my favourites, you are my favourite." But if I'm honest, a tattoo that reads "Teresa's Bitch" would really make you my favourite Kathy!

Cowboys and Broken Hearts

Lena came to the pool looking for relief from a bulging disc in her lower spine. Discs in the spine are like shock absorbers between each individual vertebra. They are ninety percent water. If you can imagine a jelly-filled donut between each bone, and over time or injury, the donuts collapse and bulge out. When this happens in the lower back, it causes pain in the buttocks and shooting pain down the legs. It is difficult and painful to treat. Movement is needed for treatment, but it is also the source of the pain. Lena had exhausted physiotherapy and pain relievers; she was desperate for help.

When she started coming to the pool, she was like a porcelain doll. She was very careful with all her moves and hesitant to try anything new that I suggested. She was fearful of spasms and making matters worse, which is very common for anyone with back issues. Over time, she made progress in the water and was willing to try new exercises with me. She started with one class a week and soon asked for another and another. In the water, she found relief for her back, but she also found a little community of people just like her. Everyone had pain shadowing their every move, but in the water, there were no shadows. For forty-five minutes, everyone felt good, and that's about all that mattered.

Lena always came in with a smile and a warm hello. She is a woman of strong faith and family ties. Despite her physical pain, she was always optimistic and soft-spoken, taking names and dates for her prayer intentions. One day at the pool, she mentioned that it was the anniversary of her son's death. I had no idea that she lost a child. I was shocked that this had never come up before. I can't imagine any pain worse than the death of a child; it changes who you are. Lena didn't seem like someone that had been "changed."

Her son's name was Ben, and he was a cowboy. He loved bull riding and rodeos, farming, family, and the great outdoors. Lena talked about Ben with tenderness and love and not with sorrow. He suffered from arthritis from a very young age, but that didn't stop him from doing all the things his heart desired. She could talk about his crazy rodeo days, terrible teenage years, and the grown man about to walk down the aisle with the woman he loved, all with a smile on her face and a heart full of pride.

He was twenty-seven years old and only a couple of months away from his wedding day when his life ended on the wrong side of a log that he had cut in the bush. I didn't know whether it was her faith, her relationship with her son, or her belief in heaven that gave her such calm. I had never met anyone like her until I met Ruthanne.

Ruthanne came to the pool looking for relief from sciatic nerve and arthritis. She had taken a fall a few months earlier and was struggling to get her mobility back. Ruthanne was in her late sixties and terrified of deep water. She needed to get on top of the pain, and she needed to keep moving to keep her independence! Ruthanne is a very independent woman!

When she started, we stayed in the shallow end; even that made her eyes wide and her heart race. Eventually, I got her to hold a noodle with me, and I would peddle her out in the deep end. I was never more than an arm's length from her, and we always had the noodle. There is nothing more rewarding in my job than to have the trust of a fearful swimmer in the water. She had a buoyancy belt on and a noodle to hold onto, but in her mind, her life was in my hands. It never was, but my heart swells, and my eyes fill to think she had that much trust in me. Ruthanne got braver as the years went on. Eventually, she didn't need me, didn't need the noodle, and tired of the belt too! I'm just waiting to see her do a cannon ball off the diving board.

We were doing a little "girl talk" at the pool one day, and Ruthanne told me about her daughter, Nikki. Nikki was born with a heart defect for which there was no cure; she would eventually need a transplant. Nikki was the only girl in the family, and she was adored by her brothers. She was beautiful and kind. She loved life and lived it well. Her heart condition worsened, and when she was thirty-three years old, she was given the choice to be put at the top of the list for a transplant. Nikki had other health complications and was already in hospital when she made a decision. The doctor told her there was a less than thirty percent chance that she would survive the surgery. She asked to be taken off the transplant list so that the next heart that became available would be offered to someone with a better survival rate. She told her family her wishes, she made her peace and gave her love to everyone, and only after she saw everyone she needed to see, she passed away.

Nikki's sacrifice is amazing. Her heart was so damaged, and yet it still beat with enough generosity and kindness to save another heart patient. Her story makes you want to be a better person (and sign your donor card!). When I heard Nilkki's story from Ruthanne, I felt like I had been touched by both of them. I was speechless as Ruthann told me how she lost her daughter and then circled right back to how she had lived: she was kind and funny and had her brothers wrapped around her little finger. I was embarrassed that I teared up while Ruthanne shared all this with me, dry-eyed. This woman had suffered greatly and still only focused on the good and happy memories.

The strength of these two women needs to be celebrated. We are all guilty of associating people with their pain. People can become bitter because life has been unkind to them, but not all do. Lena and Ruthanne have every reason to be bitter; hearts aren't meant to be broken. These are two amazing women with hearts full of love, faith, cowboys, and daughters.

What are the chances that Lena and Ruthanne would end up in the same class at our pool? My guess is that Ben, Nikki, and Karma are all watching over them, and chance had nothing to do with it.

My Overflowing Pasta Jar

Many, many moons ago, I was at Costco and found a giant glass jar of coloured pasta. I loved that jar but knew I would never eat that kind of pasta. I walked past it, then went back to get it, then put it back on the shelf again. Before I left the store, I went back to it a third time and bought the damn thing. It was part of my kitchen décor for many years; then, it was relegated to the basement. It moved from corner to corner and almost made it to a garage sale but was pulled back at the last minute. This oversize, heavy glass jar had no use in my home and yet I just couldn't bear to part with it. I threw out the pasta and kept the jar with the feeling it would have a purpose one day.

My sister Angela has three wonderful sons and one daughter, Tina. She is the baby of the family (but don't call her that!). Tina is perfect; she is sweet, kind, pretty, smart and has one extra copy of chromosome 21. I'm no scientist, but if I had to guess, chromosome 21 carries kindness and empathy because she certainly has extra of both. Tina is a sponge to other people's emotions. She has a smile that melts hearts, a gentle touch, and a never-ending supply of knock-knock jokes. Only 1 in 750 babies in Canada are born with Down Syndrome. The family of that one baby will experience a whole new kind of love. It's hard to believe just one extra chromosome can give so much to an entire family.

I was teaching aqua fit classes to a group of young adults with Down Syndrome and loving it. Their energy was high, they were always happy to see me, and their song requests ranged from ABBA to Billy Talent; this was a unique class! I decided to do a water-running marathon as a fundraiser for the London Down Syndrome Association. The association was subsidizing their classes, and this would help them keep rocking it out at the pool.

I know what you're thinking: *But Teresa, what about the pasta jar? Whatever happened to the big heavy glass jar you had in your basement for over 20 years now?!* It's an intriguing story, isn't it?

The glass jar became the donation jar for every fundraiser we have done at the pool. It's been decorated with balloons, ribbons, pictures, and signs. It started its career accepting donations for The London Down Syndrome Association, which was inspired by Tina, and then branched out to other charities. It has collected for Westover Treatment Centre, Rotary Polio Vaccines, the Terry Fox Run, Strathroy Homeless Youth, ALS, and the Gift of Life Memorial Fund. In the last seven years, that jar has collected over $ 40,000.00 from the hearts of our aqua tribe. That is a lot of money from a small group of roughly 300 people. We've hosted water-running marathons, trivia weeks, sold masks, and we even did a polar bear dip in the pool when the water was only fifty-six degrees (I wasn't sure the men that did that dip were ever going to speak to me again, but eventually Mike came around!).

The generosity of our aqua tribe is unbelievable; it amazes me how easily and freely they give not only their money but their encouragement and support. I often worry that I'm asking too often or for too much, and yet every time I ask, they give.

People are good; that's all there is to it. People are good, and I will never throw out my big glass pasta jar!

Inside Out and Backwards

My parents died very young; my dad had just turned sixty-five, and my mom was only seventy-two. Both were too young. I wasn't a child orphan or anything like that, but I felt envy for all my friends that still had parents. I couldn't help it. My dad died before my daughter was born, and my mom passed away just after my son graduated from kindergarten. My parents never saw my kids grow up, they never saw the pool get built or the career I made from it, and I never saw my parents grow old. Maybe that's why I was always afraid of growing old: I didn't have an example to follow. My best friend Karma couldn't let me age in fear. I had a village of people setting an example for me. I just had to keep my eyes open—even when I wanted to look away.

Anyone who speaks with a Dutch accent has a special place in my heart. I know it's the memory of my parents that I'm hearing, and I love it. I had a lady in my class that was eighty-three years old with a very thick Dutch accent. This woman was in great shape. She had been swimming laps three times a week for the last forty years. Yes, this was my kind of lady! She was coming to our classes in the winter when she didn't want to make the drive to London to swim laps. Her mind was as sharp as her body was strong. She was setting a great example for me and everyone else in her class.

One day she came out of the change room with her bathing suit on inside out. It happens to the best of us, but not usually with a bathing suit. A woman's one-piece bathing suit inside out looks *very* different from the right side out. There are pads and reinforcement fabric in all the right places, or when worn inside out, all the wrong places! I caught up with her before she got in the pool and gave her a heads up. She was a little embarrassed and hustled back to the change room; no harm, no foul. A few weeks later, it happened again, and again, I caught her before she got in the water. It happened once more a few weeks later, and then it became our joke. Every time she came to the pool, she would get changed and then come to me and say, "All good?" I'd give her a once over and high five to signal she was good to go. Lesson learned: inside out or right side in, laughing through a senior moment takes all the sting out of it.

One day, Carrie was teaching a class in the afternoon, and she sent me a text:

Need net. Dentures in pool.

I thought, *Damn autocorrect. I better go out and see what the hell is going on. There couldn't actually be dentures in the pool.* I went out, and most of the class, along with Carrie, were looking down at the bottom of the pool in the deep end. I joined them. Hell no, it wasn't autocorrect in her text. There were dentures, one lady with a toothless grin, and all her friends laughing away! I got the net and scooped it down to lift them. She grabbed them out of the net and popped them right in her mouth! I'm glad someone has that much faith in my water chemistry!

We have a lot of seniors in our classes, and when we started, I was intimidated by older women and worried about offending them with my colourful language or working them too hard with my style of cardio. I had nothing to worry about. These ladies had stories to share that were more colourful than mine, and they came to the pool to shake that bootie!

I'm not nervous about growing old now that I have so many good examples to follow, and I realize I had it all backwards. Growing older isn't all bad. You have confidence that allows you to share your vulnerabilities. You have knowledge and experience that makes you a great teacher. You have time to do the things you love with the people you love. If the worse that can happen is wearing your bathing suit inside out and dropping your dentures, sign me up!

Not All Heroes Wear Capes

During the COVID pandemic, the pool was closed for months at a time. It was a sad and lonely time for our aqua tribe. I started writing my Daily Love blog with links to exercise videos, healthy recipes, and of course, my stories. Our tribe stayed home, stayed strong, and when they were allowed to come back to the pool, they were ready for it. I, on the other hand, had a lot of work to do to make it happen.

The virus couldn't live in water, so the pool wasn't a problem, but everything else was. We always had eight people per class, but with distancing regulations, we had to drop it to six people per class. I had to add more classes and ask people that had been with the same group of people for years to move into new groups. Everyone understood, and I made that eight-piece puzzle fit into a six-piece frame over and over—class size, check!

We had four change rooms, and everyone took turns using them. They kept their belongings in baskets that I provided. Now everyone needed their own change room and to keep all their belongings in it during the class. I needed to build two more change rooms, so everyone had their own. We moved the equipment shelving and built two additional change rooms, check!

Our indoor pool is connected to our house through a small sunroom. You can not share the air between your house and your pool, or your house will be too humid and smell like a pool. If you came in the front door of our house, you would have no idea that there was a pool in it. This is because of that chamber room between house and pool. That chamber room was where all our aqua fitters came through. They left their coats and boots there, chatted before and after class, and warned the next class coming in of who was on deck and how hard the workout was (ya, I know what you all said about me!). This sunroom wouldn't work with COVID, it was too small for proper distancing, and it had traffic going both ways at the same time with too many contact surfaces for us to clean. I needed a vestibule built that would lead directly into the pool house but did not let the cold winter air in. We built a glass entranceway. It was all see-through, so you could have one person going through it at a time, and the next person could see when they were through and then follow one at a time and not let the cold air in. Entranceway, check!

Traffic coming and going to class was my biggest obstacle. We only had twenty minutes between classes to get one group out of the pool and the next class into the pool. In those twenty minutes, we also had to spray all the contact surfaces, rinse all the equipment and belts used, and wipe down the door handles. I couldn't have people coming and going at the same time, and we had to have the pool house empty while we sprayed contact surfaces. I had to find a way to keep people in their car (safely distanced, warm and dry) until the class before them had left and we had cleaned everything. The pool is at the back of the house, and the parking area is at the front of the house. There is no way for them to see in or for us to see them waiting. My greatest idea yet: a traffic light! Yes, an actual red-yellow-green traffic light. My electrician (another hero that doesn't wear a cape) hung and wired it to the front of the house facing the parking lot and set us up with a remote-control unit to change the light from the pool house. When the light is red, we are still getting ready, and they have to wait in their cars. When it turns green, come on in, we are ready for you!

Brilliant, you say. Damn straight it was! Now again, for the sake of keeping this book honest, before I thought of the traffic light, I had some other ideas. They were really bad, expensive ideas, and every time I came up with one and then figured out how or why it wouldn't work, I would totally lose my shit and with no boot camp classes to take out my frustrations on, my family lived in fear for a few weeks while I worked this all out in my head. No one was seriously injured during this time, but some doors were slammed, some profanities screamed, and tears shed (Ron's a crier).

It was go-time! Classes could start again, physically distanced and socially connected. Ya baby! We had been closed and isolated for four months. I was feeling a little tongue-tied about leading classes again. I had been nowhere, seen no one, done nothing; what would we talk about at classes? Well, I wasn't alone. Everyone felt socially awkward when we started up again. Normally, all our classes started with chatter about kids, grandkids, recipes, holidays and all that good stuff. Everyone came to class quiet, nervous, and fearful that they followed the rules, got in the right change room, washed their hands, and wore their masks. I had run it through in my head for months, but they hadn't, and they were scared.

We have one group of women that we call the Singing Dutch Sisters. They are a group of sisters all in their seventies and eighties that emigrated from Holland and made Canada better for it! I love these ladies. They remind me of my mom and how lively she always was. Every week they came to class, and as they arrived, they would hug and kiss; their affection for each other was honest and natural.

These ladies loved to sing during our classes. For our first day back after the shutdown, I made sure I had a sing-a-long kind of playlist. I did our warm-up to "Roll Out the Barrel." (We'll have a barrel of fun...) Not a peep from the girls. Next up was "Build Me Up, Buttercup." Nothing, nada, zip. What the hell was going on here? It was feeling like a *Twilight Zone* episode. I stopped the music and asked, "What's up? Why no singing?" They explained they're not allowed to sing at church because of the virus, so they aren't singing anywhere. That was a heartbreaker. I had thought of everything in my reopening, but I didn't think of this. Things had changed; we all had to adapt.

Therapy swims changed too. I couldn't be in the water with the group anymore. I had to stay on deck and only get in the water in case of emergency (which, as you know, we have from time to time). I had to stay distanced, which meant I couldn't dance Pam down the steps anymore. I didn't just follow the regulations for COVID, I did cartwheels and backflips over the rules, but not having Pam get back in the water was going too far. She needed to get back in the water not only for her body but for her spirits; we were her village. With a double lung transplant, she was very vulnerable to COVID, and there wasn't a vaccine available yet. She knew what precautions I had put in place, and she wanted to come back. According to the rules, she couldn't come back because she needed assistance getting in and out, and that couldn't be done with a six-foot distance. I knew what the health board rules were, but my best friend said that if I followed them, there would be a special place in hell for me one day. I don't mess with Karma. Pam was coming back to classes!

Pam had lost some strength in her legs during the lockdown. Months without water therapy, massage therapy, and physiotherapy had taken their toll on her. We had agreed that I would get her in and out of the water, and if I wasn't available, then her husband would come with her. Kudos to her husband for committing to her treatment plan, but honestly, he was no dancer! There was a very tense day when Pam was halfway up the steps and couldn't manage the two steps out or the two steps back down to the water. Bert and Tony were devising a plan to carry her out (talk about the blind leading the blind!). I was called to help. I gripped Pam, and she pushed through to the top step, hanging on me for dear life. We fired her husband and made arrangements that only Malyn and I would assist her.

Pam got stronger, the Singing Dutch Sisters started humming, and classes started to chatter again. Things were different, and so were we.

That year for Christmas, Pam gave Malyn and me cups that read, "Not All Heroes Wear Capes." Somehow, through a worldwide pandemic, I had become her hero all the while she was still mine.

Savaaaaaaaasna

Every class I teach has some cardio component in it, no matter if it's a gentle class or even the Barely Breathing class. Cardio isn't just about losing weight; it's about a healthy heart and lungs. I don't care how much you weigh. You want to breathe and keep your heart beating? Then don't be a geek—do cardio three times a week!

Most people think my favourite move is a propelled ski, but Savasana has always been my favourite. Savasana is a yoga pose that translates to corpse pose. Ya, I know. I don't like that name either, but really, that's what it is. You lie as still as possible and let your mind slow down, turn off all the chatter in your head, listen to your breath, and take a moment to feel the true power and complete calm in your body. They say Savasana is both the hardest and the easiest yoga pose. For some, they settle into it easily, while others fight it and don't know why.

At the pool, we use the noodle swings for Savasana. Everyone has a noodle that is tethered to the wall with bungee cords in a triangle. They slip in through the centre of the triangle, rest their heads on the noodle, and bring their feet to the wall to stay in place, and they float. They don't need to move or hold themselves up at all. They are completely supported by the water, the wall, and the noodle. All they have to do is stay still. Sounds easy, right? During Savasana, I move as far away from the pool as I can while still being able to see everyone. In almost every class, there is at least one person that just can't stay still. They swing their arms up and down like they're making snow angels, or they bend their knees and bounce off the wall over and over.

At my vantage point, I can see who is struggling to stay still, and I know it's not that they don't want to follow the instructions; they don't know how. For some, to stop the running, stop the music, stop all the moving pieces means to stop living. I used to be that person bouncing off the wall and making snow angels. When life has you running sixteen hours a day, taking four minutes to listen to your breath is freaking ridiculous; who has time for that shit?! If you read that last sentence and thought, *Yes, exactly. Who has time for that?* you need to read it again. Everyone has the same twenty-four hours in a day, and everyone chooses how to spend those twenty-four hours. Everyone has four minutes to listen to their own breath. Without breath, your to-do lists don't matter, what you're making for dinner won't matter, your kid's school project won't matter. Nothing matters if you don't breathe.

For the people that do stay still, it's almost like they are in a trance. Their eyebrows relax, their shoulders drop, all the wrinkles in their forehead smooth away, and with their hearts lifted, you can almost imagine all the positive energy they are taking in and storing for later. I play soft inspirational music, and at the end of the song, there is always a moment of silence while everyone gathers their thoughts to take out of the pool with them.

We have Savasana after class for one week in each session. That week, our lost and found box is overflowing. Women forget their towels, their coats, their bras, and I don't know who leaves with just one sock, but I have a handful of those too. For some, it is four minutes of bliss, and for others, it is the hardest four minutes of the class.

For me, it is a chance to sit back and look at what I've done here at the pool. I'm helping people connect the dots between body, mind, and soul. How is it a little farm girl who grew up to be a bean counter ended up here?

Karma sits beside me on the bench, and she reminds me, Teresa, just breathe.

Life Bridge

Well, we are nearing the end of our journey—no closer to the Stanley Cup than we were fifty years ago. Sorry, Leaf fans, that's going to sting a little. Don't lose hope. As long as we have a team, a coach, and the fans, there is always next year…

This last leg of our journey gives you a glimpse into what's next for the team. I'm a little nervous for the 2021–2022 season, the younger players are excited, and our final stop is for you. Whoever you are, the last page is for you. I mean it—it's just for you!

How to make a Little Bug Cry

My son, Ronny, has the kindness of Grandpa George, the generosity of Opa John, his dad's work ethic, and my funny bone, but his heart belongs to a little bug.

Ronny was a September baby, which meant he started school when he was three—he was a baby; more importantly, my baby! We had a tough transition to school. He had been home with me his whole little life, and honestly, I'm a tough act to follow! My wee little boy took that giant yellow school bus every day off to the great unknown, but every afternoon, he came home to me and Lightning.

Across the road from us was a pig farm with four grown kids and one lonesome horse named Lighting. That horse was once the love of four young kids, but as they grew up and moved on, Lightning was left to pasture. Lucky for Ronny, pasture was where the bus stopped. Every morning, we went out to wait for the bus with fear in his heart, tears in my eyes, and carrots in our pockets! Lightning loved the bus route as much as we dreaded it. In the afternoon, Lightning would come to life, galloping up and down the fence line for about ten minutes before the red flashing lights would stop traffic. Every day, Ronny got off that bus just as happy to see Lightning as he was to see me (OK, he was happier to see the horse, but he knew I packed the carrots). Ronny and Lightning had such a connection that our neighbour would ask Ronny to walk the horse back into the barn for winter and to pasture for spring. Ronny was a horse lover; he just didn't have a horse, yet.

You know how they say, "Thirty is the new twenty," meaning kids grow up much slower than we did? Our family didn't follow that rule. Our kids matured quickly. We didn't do it on purpose; it just happened that way. He worked hard, played hard, respected us, and quietly found his path to follow. All he needed was a horse.

Ronny's best friend, Zac, was dating Kate, and Kate had a sister, Michelle. Michelle had a horse named Pacman. Of course, my best friend Karma was always hanging close to Ronny; he was a good boy, but he needed a guardian angel (with a penis drawn on) to be his designated driver. Michelle and Ronny met, fell in love, and rode off into the sunset on a horse named Pacman. Well, not exactly, but great image, huh?

Ronny had a girlfriend. We wanted to meet her. OK, honestly, I *really* wanted to meet her!

Me: How about she comes for a BBQ next weekend, Ronny?

Ronny: No, she's working that weekend.

Me: How about she comes for rice and fajitas on Tuesday?

Ronny: No, she is on the night shift this week.

Me: Huh? How is that possible? She is working the weekend *and* the night shift during the week? I don't think that's legal, Ronny.

Ronny: It's confusing. She's in a union—you wouldn't understand.

Oh, I understand bullshit when I hear it, and Ronny was so full of it, his blue eyes were turning brown. My boy didn't want me to meet his girl, and that meant one thing: I had to meet her. I don't know at what age boys learn there is no point in arguing with their moms, but Ronny wasn't that old yet.

Night shift, day shift, weekends or weekdays, he just couldn't wear me down. It was finally on a Friday night that Michelle came to have dinner with the Fischtners, and she fit our family like a glove. I don't know what Ronny was worried about; the worst that could happen was that I fall in love quicker than him (I have a history of this).

After dinner, they were going shopping. It's genetic: Ronny *hates* shopping as much as I do. I asked Ronny where they were going shopping; his circuit was Canadian Tire, Sport Check, and Bass Pro Shop. You could have knocked me over with a feather when he said, "Lululemon." My boy was in love. The boy was going to lululemon?! Yeah, he was in love.

The next morning, I got up to let the dogs out. Our sweet Wally sauntered up to the front door where I noticed Michelle had forgotten her sweater. I was unlocking the door when I noticed she had also forgotten her shoes. As Wally jogged down the steps, I noticed she forgot her *car*! Oh, OK. This was happening. I could handle it. The question was, do

I let Ron roam the house for an hour in his underwear, not realizing we had an overnight guest?

Michelle became part of the family as soon as we met, and as part of the family, she needed a nickname. I believe that nicknames are a symbol of love. Michelle started every text or phone call to me with, "I don't want to bug you but…" or ended with "sorry to bug you." Truth was, this sweet little girl never bugged me. She became my Little Bug.

It is my tradition to write poems to the kids for Christmas or Birthdays or Easter or Anniversaries or for no reason at all. I love writing poems; it connects me to my mom, who wrote me the loveliest and funniest of poems. Having a poem written for you is very personal and speaks to your heart in a way that nothing else can. Michelle has a shirt that says, "If I'm not in the hospital, I'm getting back on my horse," and that is our Little Bug. She is a tough cookie. When I write a poem to someone, they have to read it aloud for everyone to hear. Michelle's poem started with, My dear Ronny Bear and Little Bug…, and that was as far as she got before the waterworks started; the poor girl couldn't even get the first verse out. It used to be the poems that made our family laugh, now we laugh harder at how quickly Michelle cries, and that, my friend, is how you make a little bug cry.

A Flower to a Butterfly

Our daughter Malyn (nickname Minnie, Minnesota, Minneapolis, Malynika, and one other that I'm not allowed to put in the book!) has a heart of gold. When teaching kids swimming lessons, she is compassionate and kind. She's patient with her grandmother and loyal to her friends. She's a good egg, my Malyn.

Recently she got a new tattoo to represent her weight loss. The tattoo is a butterfly with one wing filled in with flowers and the other is a regular butterfly wing. The wing filled with flowers represents who she was before her weight loss: she was beautiful, colourful, and made people happy. The other wing represents who she is now after her weight journey: beautiful, colourful, makes people happy, and now she can fly.

At the start of the pandemic, Malyn was so scared; it was all she could think about. A virus that no one understood or could stop from spreading brought her anxiety to a new high (and I'm not talking about the good kind of high). She got through it. We all got through it; the virus infected some and affected all. I think we are all a little different because of the pandemic. I'm finally more present and less goal-oriented. Ron and Ronny realized they could, in fact, survive one winter without NHL, Michelle found out she loves a man that will support her through anything, and Malyn learned to fly.

Malyn was the first person to read this book when it was finished. She wanted to read the chapters as I wrote them, but I wouldn't let her. She had to wait until it was done. I was thrilled to find out there were things in my book she never knew about me. She read every chapter except this one. This one she won't read until it's a published book.

When the kids were born, I bought books. *To My Son, Love, Your Mother* and *To My Daughter, Love, Your Mother*. They are books that you fill in the blanks and leave to your kids. They detail your family tree, the dates of marriages, births, deaths, etc. I bought them over twenty years ago, still have them today, and haven't filled in a single page yet. Twenty years ago, I thought those things were important.

What's important to me keeps changing; I wish I knew that twenty years ago, but I likely wouldn't have believed it. When I was younger and fainting all the time, that was about all I could think about, losing consciousness. Now I laugh while writing chapters about fainting; I never thought I could make peace with that part of my life, but I did. After all the birthday party extravaganzas I planned for my kids, I never thought I'd have the chance to shoot Ronny or that I'd want to, but I did. When my parents died, and I felt like I was left on a stage with no audience, I never thought I could go on, but I did.

Dates, marriages and names do not grow a family tree. Trees grow in the dirt, and yes, planting is messy, and pruning is hard work. Trees need water, and there will be droughts. Trees lose all their leaves in the fall and suffer through the harsh winter, and every spring, they amaze us with new growth. They do this year after year until they are so big and strong, we laugh and tell "remember when…" stories about saplings. Our family tree is still growing new branches, and let's be honest, we have some twisted roots, but we are strong and amazing.

That's what I hope Malyn takes away from this chapter. Sometimes life sucks, but it gets better. Sometimes life is awesome, and it still gets better! All your tomorrows could be great, and no matter how good or bad they are, you, Malyn, will keep flying—because you are a butterfly living in a strong tree.

What's Next?

When I started writing this book, I couldn't wait to get to the last chapter, and now that I'm here, I don't want to be. I don't like endings; I like beginnings. Sorry, my friend, you don't get an ending to this book.

As more people get vaccinated, I'm hopeful about running aqua fit classes again, along with all my pool sistas. Malyn is starting to fill the land classes and slowly but surely taking on more roles at the pool as my business partner. What started as a ripple in the water has turned into waves of happiness that I'm hoping will be splashing for years to come with more stories to tell and people to meet.

Moving forward, I want to really commit to my second marriage; no, don't worry, Ron's not going anywhere. I want to marry my careers: accounting and aqua fit. The bean counter in me still loves the world of finance. The instructor in me loves to teach. Karma has led me this far and rewarded me for following her. Time for me to give back.

During the COVID shutdown, I read an editorial in an investment magazine that I always buy. The editorial was about how the pandemic would affect future generations planning for retirement. It said the next generation would have to save much more to have the same standard of living in retirement that we will enjoy. It went on to say the only way they can possibly manage it would be to start saving much younger and much more than we did. The article said that the nest egg needed to be saved by younger generations was so big that it would overwhelm them if they knew. It's best that we not tell them. I read that article three times and got madder every time I read it. We know they need to save more and start younger, and our best way to prepare them is to *not tell them*?!

My parents taught me personal finance when I was a teenager. I taught my kids personal finance when they were teenagers. My kids will probably do the same for their kids. What would have happened if my parents didn't understand personal finance themselves? I'm sure I wouldn't have an indoor pool if not for the lessons they taught me. Personal finance is not taught in school, it's not polite to talk about socially, and after a certain age, it's just assumed you know, even if you don't. How the hell do you learn the basics of managing adult finances without someone to teach you? A lot of people don't know the difference between RRSP, RESP, TFSA or RRIF and what the advantages are to having them. With online brokerages and the ability to have self-directed savings, a whole new world of buying stocks, ETFs, mutual funds, and GICs have opened up. And it's not nearly as hard as you think.

Yes, I know what you're thinking: *Teresa, have you heard of financial advisors?* Yes, I have, and I'm not discouraging anyone from hiring one, but you need to find the right one, and to do that, you need to know the basics. Many young people are tech-savvy enough to manage their own finances, but they don't know where or how to start. If you're going to a restaurant and want to order off the menu, you need to know how to read the menu and have a basic understanding of what goes into all the dishes. Ordering food with no understanding of how it's made or what's in it can make you very sick, and investing is the same.

That's what I want to do: teach young adults the basics so they can go anywhere they want with their savings and not get sick. I want to teach for free and pay them to do their homework. I want to bridge some of the gaps between the rich and the poor. Anyone that has ever played Monopoly or Life knows the rules to the games. Now, imagine playing either of those games without ever being told the rules. You are going to lose every time you play. I want everyone to know the rules before they play, and once they do, I hope they decide to play and win often.

I'm working on a course that breaks finances down to planning an awesome road trip. Instead of ROI and interest rates, you pick a car, pick a destination, choose your route, and let's go! If they follow through with their planned trip (open an account and make a deposit), I will contribute to their first tank of gas. No ulterior motives, no strings attached—I just want everyone to know the rules to the game and to help them get started.

I don't know if anyone will even want to take this course or if I will be able to teach it effectively. It might just be an epic failure, but if I remember correctly, someone once told me, "I am the kind of woman that can do anything."

Karma is telling me to do it, and you know that bitch. Run with her or be run over.

Not The End.

A Poem for You, Whoever You Are

My mother would never forgive me if I wrote an entire book without including a single poem. This poem is written for you. Yes, you. Not just the people named in the book or the people that come to my classes. Everyone who read this book, I wrote this poem for you, whoever you are or want to be.

<u>For You</u>

I can't believe I wrote a book,
and bared my soul for you to look.

Pages filled with smiles and tears,
friends, family, hopes and fears.

Connecting words that you can feel,
with stories that inspire and heal.

My mom's humour is the ink in my pen;
Dad's love gives me the courage of ten men.

This book is part me, part you;
and of course,
part Karma too.

By,
Teresa Fischtner

Teresa Fischtner is an "aqua entrepreneur." After 25 years working in accounting, she changed careers and started teaching aquafit at her family pool. Customers come to "Over the Deep End" for full body workouts in deep water and they leave with a sense of community and friendship that Teresa has created, and all her mermaids and mermen continue to nurture.

This is Teresa's first book; she writes from her heart with honesty and humour. Comments and kindness always welcome at:

e-mail: teresa@overthedeepend.ca

 Over The Deep End

 overthedeependfitness

Special thanks to Anthony at A.H Design Photography for photos and front cover design.